Contents

W9-AUX-357

Contents

Name _____

Animal Habitats

Draw a picture of an animal on this page. Then answer the questions. (4)

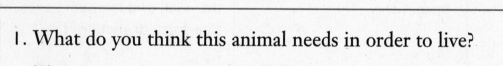

1. What do you think this animal needs in order to live?

   (2) _____

   _____

2. In what kinds of places do you think this animal could live?

   (2) _____

   _____

3. What do you like best about this animal? Why?

   (2) _____

   _____

Name _____

Animal Habitats

As you read each selection in Animal Habitats, fill in the boxes of the chart that apply to the selection. Sample answers shown.

	How do the people and animals meet?	What happens when the people and animals meet?
Nights of the Pufflings	Pufflings get lost and end up in Halla's town. **(2 points)**	Halla helps the pufflings return to the ocean. **(3)**
Seal Surfer	Ben sees the seal being born. **(2)**	Ben swims and surfs with the seal, and the seal saves Ben from drowning. **(3)**
Two Days in May	Deer come to the garden beside Sonia's apartment building. **(2)**	Sonia's neighbors make sure that the deer are safely returned to the woods. **(3)**

Assessment Tip: Total **5** Points per selection

Name _____

Bird Words

Write the correct word next to each definition. Then find and circle all seven words in the word search.

1. Holes animals use as underground nests.

   burrows **(1 point)** _____

2. To do something risky. venture **(1)** _____

3. Sending upwards like a rocket. launching **(1)** _____

4. On or to the shore. ashore **(1)** _____

5. Acting on a feeling, without thinking. instinctively **(1)** _____

6. Having no people living there. uninhabited **(1)** _____

7. Stuck or trapped. stranded **(1)** _____

Vocabulary

ashore
burrows
instinctively
launching
stranded
uninhabited
venture

Award **1 point** for completion of word search puzzle.

Name _____

Puffin Fact Chart

Why Puffins Come to the Island (page 21)	**What Growing Puffin Chicks Do (page 25)**
1. They come to raise their chicks after a winter at sea. **(2 points)**	1. They stay safely hidden in their burrows. **(1)**
2. It's spring, so it's time for them to come ashore. **(2)**	2. They call out/peep for food. **(1)**
	3. They eat fish up to ten times a day. **(1)**
What Puffins Look Like and What They Do (pages 22–23)	**What Happens on Pufflings' First Flight to the Sea (pages 28–32)**
1. They're "clowns of the sea." **(1)**	1. Many splash-land safely in the sea. **(1)**
2. They have white faces and chests and colorful beaks. **(1)**	2. Some crash-land in the village and try to hide. **(1)**
3. They tap beaks/tend eggs. **(1)**	3. Children rescue stranded pufflings and put them in boxes. **(1)**
4. They float on the ocean/catch fish. **(1)**	4. Children release the stranded pufflings on the beach. **(1)**

Answers may vary.

Assessment Tip: Total **15** Points

Name _____

The Problem with Pufflings

Finish each sentence about *Nights of the Pufflings*. Answers may vary.

1. After a winter at sea, puffins return to Halla's island because

   they want to raise their chicks there. **(2 points)**

2. Halla and her friends can't see the baby chicks because

   they are hidden inside their burrows. **(2)**

3. In August, the young pufflings come out of their burrows because

   they must fly off for their winter at sea. **(2)**

4. Pufflings that don't make it to the ocean are in danger because

   cats, dogs, cars, or trucks might hurt them. **(2)**

5. The children wander through the streets at night because

   they want to rescue the pufflings that have crash-landed in the village. **(2)**

6. The next day the children take their cardboard boxes to the beach because

   they want to release the pufflings they have rescued. **(2)**

Name _____

Fact or Opinion?

Read the story. Then go on to the next page.

A Bird by Any Other Name

Another name for a pigeon is a rock dove, and, indeed, pigeons belong to the same bird family as doves. Doves are thought to be clean, pretty, and gentle. But pigeons really look very dirty. They can be messy too!

If you live in a city, you've probably seen lots of them in parks and other places where people eat their lunch. To find food, pigeons will make pests of themselves. In some cities the return of falcons and hawks has cut down on pigeon numbers. Be glad that there are fewer pigeons around!

Some people train pigeons to fly home from many miles away. These pigeons are known as homing pigeons. They can carry messages. Scientists think that sunlight and Earth's magnetism help the pigeons know where to fly.

In the early 1800s, millions of passenger pigeons lived in North America. As settlers moved west, they hunted the birds for meat, fat, and feathers. By 1880, most passenger pigeons were gone. The last one died in a zoo in 1914. It's sad to think there are no more passenger pigeons.

Name _____

Fact or Opinion? continued

**Read each statement below. Decide if it is a fact or opinion.
Write *fact* or *opinion* on the line.**

1. Another name for a pigeon is a rock dove. <u>fact</u> **(1 point)**

2. Pigeons belong to the same family of birds as doves. <u>fact</u> **(1)**

3. Pigeons are really very dirty birds. <u>opinion</u> **(1)**

4. You can see pigeons in parks. <u>fact</u> **(1)**

5. Pigeons make pests of themselves. <u>opinion</u> **(1)**

6. You should be glad that there are fewer pigeons around. <u>opinion</u> **(1)**

7. Homing pigeons can carry messages. <u>fact</u> **(1)**

8. The last passenger pigeon died in 1914. <u>fact</u> **(1)**

9. It's sad that there are no more passenger pigeons. <u>opinion</u> **(1)**

How did you figure out which of the statements above were opinions?
Write a sentence to explain your thinking.

<u>They could not be proven true.</u> **(1)**

_____

Name _____

Dictionary Disaster

The writers of this dictionary page need your help. They have included each word, its part of speech, and its definition. Now finish each entry by dividing the word into syllables.

Example: notebook *noun* A book with blank pages to write on.

note • book

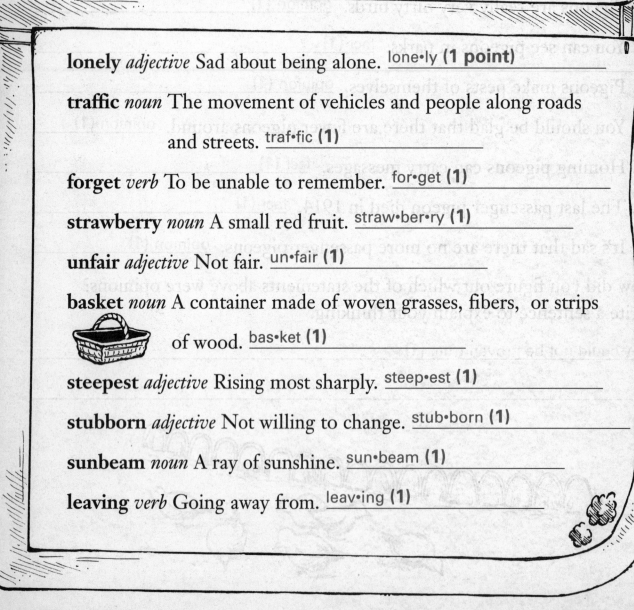

lonely *adjective* Sad about being alone. lone•ly **(1 point)**

traffic *noun* The movement of vehicles and people along roads and streets. traf•fic **(1)**

forget *verb* To be unable to remember. for•get **(1)**

strawberry *noun* A small red fruit. straw•ber•ry **(1)**

unfair *adjective* Not fair. un•fair **(1)**

basket *noun* A container made of woven grasses, fibers, or strips of wood. bas•ket **(1)**

steepest *adjective* Rising most sharply. steep•est **(1)**

stubborn *adjective* Not willing to change. stub•born **(1)**

sunbeam *noun* A ray of sunshine. sun•beam **(1)**

leaving *verb* Going away from. leav•ing **(1)**

Assessment Tip: Total **10** Points

Name _____

The Vowel + /r/ Sounds in *hair*

There are three different ways to spell the /âr/ sounds heard in *hair*. The three patterns are as follows:

are, as in c**are**

air, as in h**air**

ear, as in b**ear**

► In the starred word *where,* the /âr/ sounds are spelled *ere.*

Write each Spelling Word under its spelling of the /âr/ sounds. Order of answers for each category may vary.

Spelling Words

1. hair
2. care
3. chair
4. pair
5. bear
6. where*
7. scare
8. air
9. pear
10. bare
11. fair
12. share

are

care **(1 point)**

scare **(1)**

bare **(1)**

share **(1)**

air

hair **(1)**

chair **(1)**

pair **(1)**

air **(1)**

fair **(1)**

ear

bear **(1)**

pear **(1)**

Another Spelling

where **(1)**

Theme 4: **Animal Habitats**   9
Assessment Tip: Total **12** Points

Name _____

Spelling Spree

Hink Pinks **Write the Spelling Word that fits the clue and rhymes with the given word.**

Example: a purchase during an **sky** _buy_
airplane flight

1. a long look by a large, furry animal _____ **stare**
2. a rip in a seat cushion _____ **tear**
3. a hairless rabbit _____ **hare**
4. taking care of a female horse **mare** _____
5. products made from animal fur _____ **ware**
6. a challenge to eat a fruit _____ **dare**
7. a frightening-looking costume _____ **wear**

1. _bear **(1 point)**_   5. _hair **(1)**_

2. _chair **(1)**_   6. _pear **(1)**_

3. _bare **(1)**_   7. _scare **(1)**_

4. _care **(1)**_

Spelling Words
1. hair
2. care
3. chair
4. pair
5. bear
6. where*
7. scare
8. air
9. pear
10. bare
11. fair
12. share

Letter Swap **Change the underlined letter in each word to make a Spelling Word. Write the Spelling Word.**

Example: would *could*

8. fai_l_   _fair **(1)**_   11. fi_r_   _air **(1)**_

9. _t_here   _where **(1)**_   12. pai_d_   _pair **(1)**_

10. sha_p_e   _share **(1)**_

Assessment Tip: Total **12** Points

Name _____

Proofreading and Writing

Proofreading **Circle the five misspelled Spelling Words. Then write each word correctly.**

Iceland at a Glance

Iceland is an island in the Atlantic Ocean. Most visitors arrive by (aer.) Few travel to the center of the island, (whare) glaciers cover most of the land. Even the coastal areas are almost (bair) of trees. The people of Iceland take (kare) to make visitors feel welcome. They are happy to (shear) their favorite foods with you. If you go to this unusual island, you'll enjoy your visit!

Spelling Words

1. hair
2. care
3. chair
4. pair
5. bear
6. where*
7. scare
8. air
9. pear
10. bare
11. fair
12. share

1. air **(1 point)**

2. where **(1)**

3. bare **(1)**

4. care **(1)**

5. share **(1)**

Write a Notice The children of Heimaey Island do their best to rescue the lost pufflings. You want to help by writing a notice warning people to watch out for the young birds. How would you get people's attention? What would you ask them to do?

On a separate sheet of paper, write a notice to the people of Heimaey Island. Use Spelling Words from the list. Responses will vary. **(5)**

Theme 4: **Animal Habitats**   11
Assessment Tip: Total **10** Points

Name the Part of Speech

**Read each sentence. Decide the part of speech for each
underlined word. Then choose the correct meaning. Write
the correct letter in the blank.**

1. Halla <u>spots</u> her first puffin of the season. __b (2)__
   a. *noun* Small marks or stains.
   b. *verb* Finds or locates.

2. The puffins <u>land</u> while the children are in school. __b (2)__
   a. *noun* The part of Earth not covered by water.
   b. *verb* To come down on a surface.

3. Many puffins ride the <u>waves</u> that are close to shore. __a (2)__
   a. *noun* Ridges or swells moving across a body of water.
   b. *verb* Flaps or flutters.

4. Halla's friend <u>spies</u> a puffin overhead. __b (2)__
   a. *noun* Secret agents who get information about an enemy.
   b. *verb* Catches sight of; sees.

5. The pufflings cannot take off from flat <u>ground</u>. __a (2)__
   a. *noun* The solid surface of the earth; land.
   b. *verb* To cause to touch the bottom of a body of water.

6. Halla wishes the little birds a safe <u>journey</u>. __a (2)__
   a. *noun* A trip; a passage from one place to another.
   b. *verb* To make a journey.

Name _____

Completing with *be*

Complete each sentence. Fill in the blank with the form of *be* that matches the subject. Use the tense named in parentheses.

1. The story __is (1 point)__ about pufflings. (present)

2. We __are (1)__ curious about these birds. (present)

3. The pufflings __were (1)__ beautiful. (past)

4. Halla __was (1)__ ready. (past)

5. She __is (1)__ very clever. (present)

6. The birds __are (1)__ confused by the village lights. (present)

7. Children __were (1)__ everywhere, searching for lost birds. (past)

8. One small puffling __was (1)__ stranded in the village. (past)

9. The students __were (1)__ very brave. (past)

10. I __am (1)__ glad they rescued the pufflings. (present)

Name _____

Be-ing Smart

The Irregular Verb *be*		
Subject	**Present**	**Past**
I	am	was
you	are	were
he, she, it, singular noun	is	was
we, they	are	were
plural noun	are	were

Use the verbs in the chart to complete these sentences.
Cross off each verb in the chart when you use it.

1. The puffin <u>is (1 point)</u> a beautiful bird. (am, is)

2. I <u>am (1)</u> sorry that some get stranded. (am, are)

3. You <u>were (1)</u> very helpful during the rescue. (was, were)

4. The students <u>are (1)</u> heroes. (are, am)

5. We <u>were (1)</u> surprised by the number of pufflings. (was, were)

6. I <u>was (1)</u> almost frightened by the strange noises. (was, were)

7. The puffling's cry <u>was (1)</u> sad. (were, was)

8. The young birds <u>were (1)</u> hungry. (was, were)

9. You <u>are (1)</u> curious about pufflings. (is, are)

10. They <u>are (1)</u> fascinating animals. (are, is)

Assessment Tip: Total **10** Points

Name _____

Forms of the Verb *be*

Good writers are careful to use the correct form of the verb *be*.
When the verb is correct, the subject of the sentence and the
verb match.

Rewrite the postcard. Correct the forms of *be*. (1 point for each verb)

> Dear Elena,
>
> Hello from Iceland. You was right! This vacation
> were really amazing. The pufflings is the cutest birds.
>
> We was outside one night. We heard a small cry.
> The sound be very sad. It be a little peep-peep-peep.
>
> Two little pufflings was stranded in the street. We caught
> them in a box. The night were very cold, but we didn't care.
> We let the birds go at the beach. They was so happy
> near the ocean. We was happy too.
>
> See you soon,
> Marcia

Dear Elena, _____

    Hello from Iceland. You **were** right! This vacation **was** really amazing.

The pufflings **are** the cutest birds.

    We **were** outside one night. We heard a small cry. The sound **is** very sad. It **is**

a little peep-peep-peep.

    Two little pufflings **were** stranded in the street. We caught them in a

box. The night **was** very cold, but we didn't care. We let the birds go at the

beach. They **were** so happy near the ocean. We **were** happy too.

      See you soon,

      Marcia

Name _____

Taking Notes

Read this passage to find out more about Iceland.

The Land of the Midnight Sun

Iceland is a country that is also a large island. It is very far north, close to the Arctic Circle, in the North Atlantic Ocean. For two months in the winter, it is dark all the time, except for four to six hours of light a day. But in June, it is daylight all the time. There is no night at all. That is why Iceland is called "The Land of the Midnight Sun."

Even though Iceland is very far north, it is not as cold as you might expect. Most people in Iceland live on the coast. Warm winds from the sea keep the coast from getting very cold. The winters are mild compared to the winters in the northern United States and Canada. The summers in Iceland are cool. The temperature is more like spring than the hot summers most Americans and Canadians are used to.

Take notes on the passage and write them in the outline below.

Iceland

What is it? a country that is an island **(2 points)**

Where is it? near the Arctic Circle in the North Atlantic Ocean **(2)**

Why is it called "The Land of the Midnight Sun"? It is called "The Land of

the Midnight Sun" because it is daylight all day in June. There is no nighttime then.

For two months in winter, there are only four to six hours of daylight. **(6)**

What is the weather like? Winters are milder than in the northern U.S. or

Canada. Summers are cooler and more like spring. **(4)**

Assessment Tip: Total **14** Points

Name _____

Choosing What's Important

Read this passage. Then answer the questions below.

Natural Wonders of Iceland

The inner part of Iceland has few people but many wonders of nature.

Volcanoes A volcano is an opening in the earth over very hot melted rock. It gives off a gas that pushes up through the opening and makes a big explosion. *Iceland has over 200 volcanoes.*

Geysers Geysers are hot springs that throw streams of water into the air. The word *geyser* comes from *Geysir,* the most famous natural fountain in Iceland.

A trip to Iceland would show you many wonders of nature.

1. What do the two subheadings tell about the title?

   They tell what some natural wonders of Iceland are. **(2 points)**

2. Look at the last sentence under "Volcanoes." Why

   do you think it is in slanted letters? It is in slanted letters to

   call attention to it because it is important information. **(2)**

3. Which two words appear in slanted type under "Geysers"? Why?

   The first is a word being defined and the second is the name of a place. **(2)**

4. What does the picture show? It shows a volcano exploding.

   Smoke and melted rock are coming out of the top. **(2)**

5. What information is repeated in the last paragraph? The last paragraph

   repeats the main idea. **(2)**

Name _____

Revising Your Research Report

Reread your story. What do you need to make it better? Use this page to help you decide. Put a checkmark in the box for each sentence that describes your personal narrative.

Rings the Bell!

☐ I chose an interesting topic to research.

☐ I used different sources to find information on the topic.

☐ My paragraphs have topic sentences and supporting facts.

☐ My ending sums up what I found out.

☐ There are almost no mistakes.

Getting Stronger

☐ I could make the topic more interesting for the reader.

☐ More sources would make sure I have the facts right.

☐ I could add some supporting details to my paragraphs.

☐ I need a better ending.

☐ There are a few mistakes.

Try Harder

☐ My topic isn't very interesting.

☐ I didn't use enough sources to find my facts.

☐ I don't have topic sentences for my paragraphs, and I'm missing many supporting details.

☐ There are a lot of mistakes.

Name _____

Subject-Verb Agreement

Circle the correct form of each verb.

1. Lizards (is/**are**) the largest group in the reptile family. (**1 point**)

2. The Komodo dragon (**is**/are) the largest lizard. (**1**)

3. The Komodo dragon (measure/**measures**) up to 10 feet in length. (**1**)

4. Lizards (lives/**live**) in every kind of habitat except the ocean. (**1**)

5. All reptiles (**are**/is) cold-blooded. (**1**)

6. A cold-blooded animal (do/**does**) not make its own body heat. (**1**)

7. To warm its blood, a lizard (bask/**basks**) in the sun. (**1**)

8. I (**own**/owns) a lizard called a swift. (**1**)

9. The swift (move/**moves**) slowly when it is cold. (**1**)

10. Then I (**turn**/turns) on a heat lamp. (**1**)

11. Suddenly, the swift (**runs**/run) very fast. (**1**)

12. At night, lizards (**hide**/hides) to stay away from enemies. (**1**)

Name _____

Spelling Words

Look for spelling patterns you have learned to help you remember the Spelling Words on this page. Think about the parts that you find hard to spell.

Write the missing letters in the Spelling Words below.

1. girl
2. they
3. want
4. was
5. into
6. who
7. our
8. new
9. would
10. could
11. a lot
12. buy

1. c __o__ __u__ __l__ d **(1 point)**

2. __a__ lot **(1)**

3. b __u__ y **(1)**

4. __o__ __u__ r **(1)**

5. w __o__ __u__ __l__ d **(1)**

6. n __e__ __w__ **(1)**

7. __w__ __h__ o **(1)**

8. g __i__ __r__ l **(1)**

9. w __a__ nt **(1)**

10. in __t__ __o__ **(1)**

11. w __a__ __s__ **(1)**

12. th __e__ __y__ **(1)**

Study List On another sheet of paper, write each Spelling Word. Check the list to be sure you spell each word correctly.

Order of words may vary. **(2)**

Assessment Tip: Total **14** Points

Name _____

Spelling Spree

Opposites Switch **Write the Spelling Word that means the opposite of each underlined word or words.**

1–2. I <u>wouldn't</u> be able to run much faster if I <u>couldn't</u> find a pair of shoes that fit.

3–4. The <u>old</u> parents named their baby <u>boy</u> Sue.

5–6. It takes a <u>little</u> of money to <u>sell</u> a boat that big.

7–8. I <u>wasn't</u> going <u>out of</u> the park when I saw smoke coming from a nearby house.

1–2. would, could **(2 points)** _____

3–4. new, girl **(2)** _____

5–6. a lot, buy **(2)** _____

7–8. was, into **(2)** _____

Letter Math **Add and subtract letters from the words below to make Spelling Words. Write the new words.**

9. out – t + r = our **(1)** _____

10. then – n + y = they **(1)** _____

11. while – ile + o = who **(1)** _____

12. slant – sl + w = want **(1)** _____

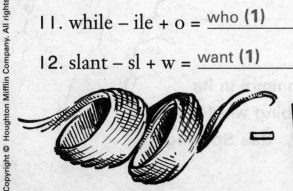

Theme 4: **Animal Habitats**   21
Assessment Tip: Total **12 Points**

Name _____

Proofreading and Writing

Proofreading Circle the four misspelled Spelling Words in this announcement. Then write each word correctly.

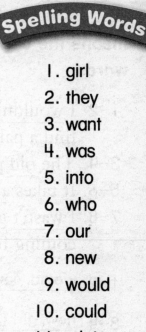

The State Zoo is proud to announce a (noo) approach to exhibiting our animals. Each animal's home is now more like the habitat (thay) would find in the wild. We think that the change will make (alot) of difference in the lives of the animals. And after all, we (wont) the animals to feel that this is their home!

1. new **(2 points)**   3. a lot **(2)**

2. they **(2)**   4. want **(2)**

Describe a Habitat Draw a picture of an animal in its habitat. Then write a few sentences describing what you drew. The animal can be real or imaginary. Use Spelling Words from the list. **(2)**

Beach Crossword

Name _____

Complete the crossword puzzle using the words from the box.

Across

2. a dock **(1 point)**
3. dived downward **(1)**
4. rested in warmth **(1)**
6. a long, rolling wave **(1)**
7. the line where earth and sky meet **(1)**

Down

1. struck against powerfully **(1)**
5. sea animal with fur and flippers **(1)**
6. waves, or to ride on waves **(1)**

Vocabulary

basked
buffeted
horizon
quay
surf
swell
seal
swooped

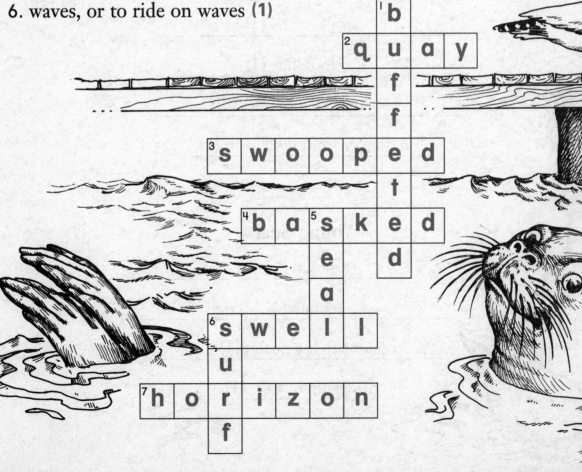

Theme 4: **Animal Habitats**   23
Assessment Tip: Total **8** Points

Name _____

Venn Diagram

Accept varied answers.

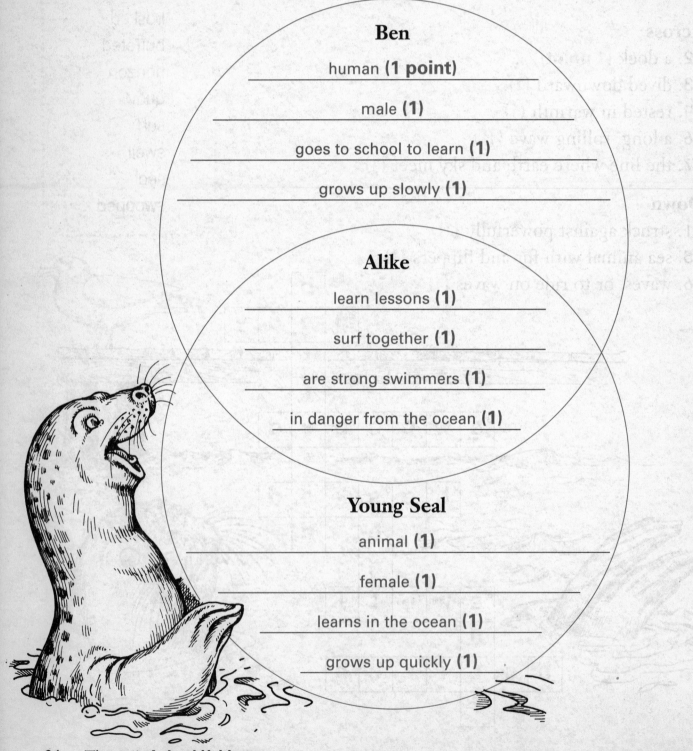

Ben

human **(1 point)**

male **(1)**

goes to school to learn **(1)**

grows up slowly **(1)**

Alike

learn lessons **(1)**

surf together **(1)**

are strong swimmers **(1)**

in danger from the ocean **(1)**

Young Seal

animal **(1)**

female **(1)**

learns in the ocean **(1)**

grows up quickly **(1)**

Assessment Tip: Total **12** Points

Name _____

Ben's Diary

Suppose Ben kept a diary. Help him finish this page by completing the sentences with details from *Seal Surfer*. Answers may vary slightly.

> One day when Granddad and I were on the beach, we
> found <u>a mother seal and her pup **(2 points)**</u>.
> That summer I watched as <u>the pup grew up and learned to swim **(2)**</u>
> _____. All winter, my young
> seal friend <u>learned how to live in the sea **(2)**</u>.
> When spring came, I thought my seal friend <u>had died **(2)**</u>
> _____. Then she returned one summer day
> when I was surfing. When I started to drown, she helped me by
> <u>pushing me up to the surface, saving me **(2)**</u>.
> I knew we would be friends forever!

Name _____

Different and Alike

**Read the story. Then complete the
diagram on the next page.**

Which Kind to Choose?

When Linda and Tracy learned
they could each get a dog, the two
friends found the dog books in the
library. Then they started reading. Some
time later, Linda said, "I'd like a dog that's
friendly, loving, and loyal. Oh, and you know, my
great-grandmother lives with us. She can't get out much,
so we want a small dog to sit with her in the day. Also, it
shouldn't need too much outdoor exercise."

Tracy said, "This book says toy poodles don't need a lot of
exercise. They're also loving and like to be cuddled. And they
need to be brushed every day."

"A small poodle sounds perfect for my family," Linda said.
"What kind of dog is your family looking for?"

"You've seen how big our yard is," Tracy responded. "And
my family loves to hike, so we're looking for a big dog that
enjoys the outdoors and can keep up with us!"

"How about a Labrador retriever?" asked Linda. "It says
that they love the outdoors, long walks, and exercise. They
don't need as much grooming as other dogs."

"They're beautiful," Tracy said, looking at the picture.
"My family would love one. But I wonder if they're friendly
and loyal."

"It says they are," Linda said, looking at the book.

The girls smiled at each other and talked about dogs for
hours! Which dog did each one choose? Guess!

Name _____

Different and Alike continued

Complete the diagram with details from the story.

Toy Poodles

small **(1 point)**

don't need a lot of exercise **(1)**

need to be brushed every day **(1)**

Similarities

friendly **(1)**

loyal **(1)**

_____

Labrador Retrievers

big **(1)**

need outdoor exercise **(1)**

don't need too much grooming **(1)**

Which dog would you choose — a poodle or a Labrador retriever? Why?

Answers will vary. **(2)**

_____

Name _____

Happy Endings

**Complete the story by filling in the blanks. Build each word by
adding either *-ed* or *-ing* to the word in dark type. Remember,
when a base word ends with a consonant and *y*, change the
y to *i* before adding *-ed*.**

As Ellie walked beneath the maple tree, she heard a noise from

above. Ellie **(look)** looked **(1 point)** _____ up and spotted a nest

with two baby robins inside. The young birds **(cry)**

cried **(1)** _____ out, "Cheep! Cheep!"

"Why are you crying?" Ellie asked the noisy birds. She **(try)**

tried **(1)** _____ to figure out the problem. "Are you

hungry?" she wondered.

"Cheep! Cheep!" the birds **(reply)** replied **(1)** _____ .

Ellie **(start)** started **(1)** _____ **(worry)** worrying **(1)** _____

that the mother robin would not return. She hoped the mother bird was

(hurry) hurrying **(1)** _____ back with food.

Suddenly, the mother robin appeared. She

(empty) emptied **(1)** _____ a beak full of worms into the

mouths of her hungry babies. The young birds began **(chirp)**

chirping **(1)** _____ sweetly. It was very **(satisfy)**

satisfying **(1)** _____ to see the birds so happy.

Name _____

Adding Endings

A **base word** is a word to which an ending may be added. When a base word ends with *e*, drop the *e* before adding *-ed* or *-ing*. When a base word ends with one vowel and one consonant, the consonant is usually doubled before *-ed* or *-ing* is added.

care − e + ed = car**ed**   grin + n + ing = gri**nning**

▶ In the starred word *fixing*, the *x* in *fix* is not doubled before *-ing* is added.

When a base word ends with a consonant and *y*, change the *y* to *i* before adding *-es* or *-ed*.

baby − y + ies = bab**ies**

Write each Spelling Word under the heading that shows what happens to the base word when an ending is added. Order of answers for each category may vary.

Spelling Words

1. cared
2. babies
3. chopped
4. saving
5. carried
6. fixing*
7. hurried
8. joking
9. grinning
10. smiled
11. wrapped
12. parties

Final *e* Dropped

cared **(1 point)**

saving **(1)**

joking **(1)**

smiled **(1)**

y Changed to *i*

babies **(1)**

carried **(1)**

hurried **(1)**

parties **(1)**

Final Consonant Doubled

chopped **(1)**

grinning **(1)**

wrapped **(1)**

No Spelling Change

fixing **(1)**

Assessment Tip: Total **12** Points

Name _____

Spelling Spree

Words in Words Write the Spelling Words that contain each of the smaller words below.

Spelling Words

Example: top _____ *stopped*

1. king   joking **(1 point)**

2. rap   wrapped **(1)**

3. are   cared **(1)**

4. grin   grinning **(1)**

5. hop   chopped **(1)**

6. mile   smiled **(1)**

1. cared
2. babies
3. chopped
4. saving
5. carried
6. fixing*
7. hurried
8. joking
9. grinning
10. smiled
11. wrapped
12. parties

Classifying Write the Spelling Word that belongs in each group.

Example: forming, creating, _____ *making*

7. moved, transported, _____

8. infants, toddlers, _____

9. repairing, mending, _____

10. raced, rushed, _____

11. celebrations, get-togethers, _____

12. keeping, storing, _____

7. carried **(1)**

8. babies **(1)**

9. fixing **(1)**

10. hurried **(1)**

11. parties **(1)**

12. saving **(1)**

Assessment Tip: Total **12** Points

Name _____

Proofreading and Writing

Proofreading **Circle the five misspelled Spelling Words in the following journal entry. Then write each word correctly.**

October 10—I fished all morning. Then I (hurryed) back to the harbor to meet Ben. We saw a female seal swimming in the harbor water. She looked like she was (grining) at us. I (choped) up some fish and tossed it to her. The seal ate the fish right away. Ben smiled and said, "I guess she's not interested in (saveing) the fish for later." The seal swam away. We (wraped) up the rest of our fish and brought it home. I wonder if we'll see that seal again.

Spelling Words

1. cared
2. babies
3. chopped
4. saving
5. carried
6. fixing*
7. hurried
8. joking
9. grinning
10. smiled
11. wrapped
12. parties

1. hurried **(2 points)**   4. saving **(2)**

2. grinning **(2)**   5. wrapped **(2)**

3. chopped **(2)**

Write About an Animal Do you have a favorite animal story? Maybe you know a funny story about a pet. Perhaps you have seen a rare or unusual animal in a zoo or aquarium. Maybe you have read a book or seen a TV program about an animal that did something remarkable.

On a separate sheet of paper, write a paragraph about an interesting animal. Use Spelling Words from the list. Responses will vary **(2)**

Name _____

Find the Right Word, the Right Meaning

Read each sentence. Then choose the correct meaning of the underlined word from the dictionary definitions below. Write the number of the correct entry and the correct meaning next to the sentence.

bit ¹ *noun* **1.** A tiny piece: *I ate the last bit of fish.* **2.** A small amount of time: *The train will come in a bit.* **3.** A small role, as in a play.
bit ¹ (bĭt) ◇ *noun, plural* **bits**
bit ² *noun* **1.** A drilling tool. **2.** The metal mouthpiece of a bridle, used to control a horse.
bit ² (bĭt) ◇ *noun, plural* **bits**
bit ³ *verb* Past tense and a past participle of **bite.**
bit ³ (bĭt) ◇ *verb*

1. The rider put the <u>bit</u> and the saddle on the horse.

   bit ², definition 2 **(2 points)** _____

2. I'll go to the movies with you in a <u>bit</u>.

   bit ¹, definition 2 **(2)** _____

3. The wood was so hard that it snapped the carpenter's <u>bit</u>.

   bit ², definition 1 **(2)** _____

4. We <u>bit</u> into the sweet apples.

   bit ³ **(2)** _____

5. There was just a <u>bit</u> of salad left after dinner.

   bit ¹, definition 1 **(2)** _____

Assessment Tip: Total **10** Points

Name _____

Finding Helping Verbs

**Circle the helping verb in each sentence. Underline the
verb that it is helping.**

1. Ben (has) <u>watched</u> the seals. **(1 point)**

2. We (have) <u>listened</u> to the waves. **(1)**

3. The waves (have) <u>buffeted</u> the seals. **(1)**

4. The seals (have) <u>arrived</u> safely. **(1)**

5. Grandfather (has) <u>talked</u> with Ben. **(1)**

6. He (has) <u>explained</u> many mysteries of the sea. **(1)**

7. The waves (have) <u>crashed</u> into the shore. **(1)**

8. One seal (has) <u>rescued</u> Ben. **(1)**

9. She (has) <u>helped</u> him. **(1)**

10. You (have) <u>learned</u> about seals. **(1)**

Name _____

Completing with Helping Verbs

Write *have* or *has* to complete each sentence.

1. We __have **(1 point)**__ learned about seals.

2. Seals __have **(1)**__ basked in the sun.

3. It __has **(1)**__ warmed the seals.

4. Grandfather __has **(1)**__ played Beethoven for seals.

5. They __have **(1)**__ listened to the music.

6. Ben __has **(1)**__ surfed with seals.

7. He __has **(1)**__ watched one of the seals grow up.

8. She __has **(1)**__ returned every year.

9. I __have **(1)**__ enjoyed learning about seals.

10. You __have **(1)**__ discovered many new facts.

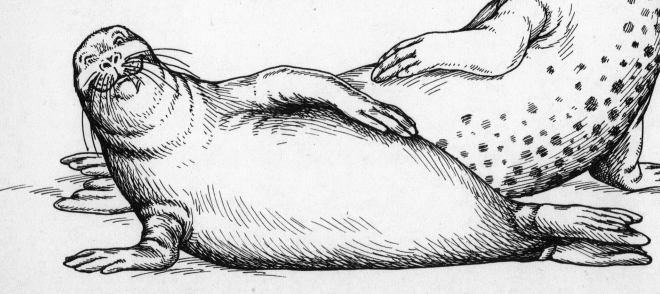

Assessment Tip: Total **10** Points

Name _____

Sentence Combining with Helping Verbs

Use helping verbs to combine each pair of sentences.

1. We have studied seals. We have discovered how they live.

   We have studied seals and discovered how they live. **(1 point)**

2. A storm has started. A storm has threatened some seals.

   A storm has started and threatened some seals. **(1)**

3. The seals have dived deep. The seals have escaped.

   The seals have dived deep and escaped. **(1)**

4. Ben's seal has returned. Ben's seal has recognized him right away.

   Ben's seal has returned and recognized him right away. **(1)**

5. The waves have pushed Ben off his board. The waves have pulled him under.

   The waves have pushed Ben off his board and pulled him under. **(1)**

6. A seal has pushed Ben up. A seal has saved him.

   A seal has pushed Ben up and saved him. **(1)**

7. I have finished the story. I have cried at the ending.

   I have finished the story and cried at the ending. **(1)**

8. Grandfather and Ben have watched the seals. Grandfather and Ben have admired the seals.

   Grandfather and Ben have watched and admired the seals. **(1)**

Theme 4: **Animal Habitats**   35
Assessment Tip: Total **8 Points**

Name _____

Planning a Poem

**Use this graphic organizer to plan a poem of your own.
Then write a poem about an experience you have had with
an animal, or a place that you like very much.**

<table>
<tr>
<td>

**Sense Words
I Might Use**

(2 points) _____

_____

_____

</td>
<td>

**Unusual Comparisons
I Might Use**

(2) _____

_____

_____

</td>
</tr>
</table>

What Is the Big Picture I Want to Create?

(2) _____

_____

_____

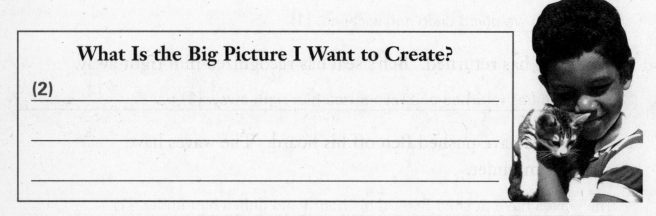

<table>
<tr>
<td>

**Rhythm Patterns
I Might Use**

(2) _____

_____

_____

</td>
<td>

**How I Might
Organize the Poem**

(2) _____

_____

_____

</td>
</tr>
</table>

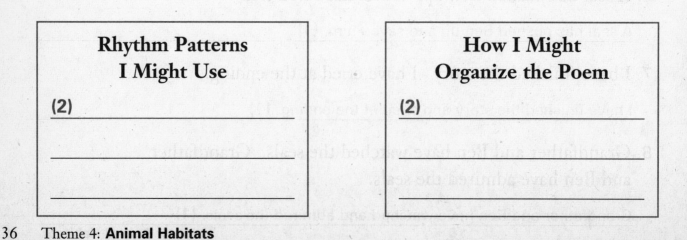

Assessment Tip: Total **10** Points

Name _____

Using Exact Verbs

Good writers try not to use a general verb when they can choose
an exact verb to describe an action. Read these examples:

Wildflowers appeared on the rugged cliffs.
Wildflowers **bloomed** on the rugged cliffs.

The rough waves threw the seals against the rocks.
The rough waves **dashed** the seals against the rocks.

**Read the sentences below. Then rewrite them, replacing
each underlined word with an exact verb.**
Answers will vary. Possible responses shown.

1. The face of the seal suddenly <u>showed</u> through the water.

   The face of the seal suddenly **emerged** through the water. **(2 points)**

   _____

2. The seal's shiny body <u>swam</u> in the water.

   The seal's shiny body **flashed** in the water. **(2)**

   _____

3. The boy's body <u>dropped</u> into the darkness of the sea.

   The boy's body **sank** into the darkness of the sea. **(2)**

   _____

4. The boy <u>moved head over heels</u> through the surf.

   The boy **somersaulted** through the surf. **(2)**

5. The seal <u>put</u> the boy onto his surfboard.

   The seal **flipped** the boy onto his surfboard. **(2)**

Theme 4: **Animal Habitats**   37
Assessment Tip: Total **10** Points

Name _____

Oh, Deer!

**You are a scientist observing a small group of deer.
The deer are eating grass in a field near a forest of
trees. Deer have never been seen in this field before.
Use the Vocabulary Words to write sentences about
the deer. If you need help, use your glossary.**

(**2 points** for each word used correctly)

Vocabulary
grazing
population
starve
surrounding
territory
wander

Assessment Tip: Total **12** Points

Name _____

Decision Chart

Problem: There are deer in the city. **(2 points)**

_____

_____

Answers may vary. Sample answers provided.

Do you agree with how the characters solve the problem?	
Yes, when...	**No, when...**
Sonia tells Mr. Donovan about the deer.	neighbors first gather around the deer.
Papa calls the animal control officer.	Papa and Mr. Donovan talk only to each other.
the group decides to gather around the deer to protect them.	they offer pizza to Mr. Scully.
Mr. Benny calls the wildlife rescue organization.	Sonia is allowed to sleep outside. **(5)**
the group doesn't leave after the animal control officer arrives.	
the neighbors spend the night outside. **(5)**	

Name _____

Oh, Deer Me!

**Write the following story events on the
lines below in the order they occurred.**

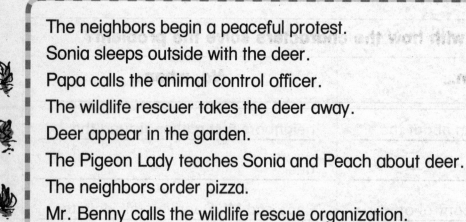

The neighbors begin a peaceful protest.
Sonia sleeps outside with the deer.
Papa calls the animal control officer.
The wildlife rescuer takes the deer away.
Deer appear in the garden.
The Pigeon Lady teaches Sonia and Peach about deer.
The neighbors order pizza.
Mr. Benny calls the wildlife rescue organization.

1. Deer appear in the garden. **(1 point)**

2. Papa calls the animal control officer. **(1)**

3. The Pigeon Lady teaches Sonia and Peach about deer. **(1)**

4. The neighbors begin a peaceful protest. **(1)**

5. Mr. Benny calls the wildlife rescue organization. **(1)**

6. The neighbors order pizza. **(1)**

7. Sonia sleeps outside with the deer. **(1)**

8. The wildlife rescuer takes the deer away. **(1)**

Assessment Tip: Total **8** Points

Name _____

What's Best for the Neighbors?

All the neighbors must decide what to plant in the neighborhood garden. Read the dialogue. Then answer the questions on the next page.

Mrs. Rhonda: Let's grow tomatoes again. They can be canned, and we can freeze tomato sauce.

Luis: Sure, and everyone likes pizza sauce. I vote for potatoes as well. If we store them in a cool place, we can use them all winter.

Blossom: But potatoes are so cheap to buy at the store! They take too much room. I'd rather have more space for lettuce and spinach.

Mr. Yost: But I don't like spinach.

Blossom: We can plant beans and peas around the fence. That's easy enough. Then the center can be used for lettuce, spinach, and tomatoes.

Mrs. Rhonda: Shall we plant squash this year?

Luis: Squash always takes over the garden. If we plant three zucchini plants, we'll have thousands of zucchini, and we'll never use it all. It's a waste.

Mr. Yost: But zucchini bread tastes good.

Mrs. Rhonda: Here's an idea. We'll plant just one zucchini plant over here, and we can set potatoes all around it. That way, all the vines will be in the same area. Then we can plant the salad greens together and the peas and beans together too.

Name _____

What's Best for the Neighbors? continued

Answer each question about the neighborhood meeting.

1. What good points does Mrs. Rhonda make in favor of planting tomatoes?

   They can be canned and made into sauce. **(2 points)**

2. What good point does Luis make in favor of planting potatoes?

   Potatoes can be used all winter long. **(2)**

3. What two good points does Blossom make against growing potatoes?

   They're cheap to buy at the store, and they take up too much room. **(2)**

4. Whose points are not well backed by facts?

   Mr. Yost's **(2)**

5. Do you agree with Mrs. Rhonda's ideas for the garden? Why or why not?

   Answers will vary. **(2)**

Assessment Tip: Total **10** Points

Name _____

What's the Word?

Prefix	Meaning	Example
un-	"not" or "the opposite of"	unable
re-	"again" or "back to"	rebuild

Suffix	Meaning	Example
-ful	"full of" or "having the qualities of"	cheerful
-er	"one who"	teacher
-ly	"in this way"	gently

Read each clue and unscramble the answer.

1. fill again: **LELRIF** — refill **(1 point)**

2. in a kind way: **DLNKYI** — kindly **(1)**

3. someone who announces: **NEURNACON** — announcer **(1)**

4. not clear: **ACNRLEU** — unclear **(1)**

5. full of beauty: **LABUTUFIE** — beautiful **(1)**

6. appear again: **PERAEPRA** — reappear **(1)**

7. full of help: **HPLELUF** — helpful **(1)**

8. someone who sings: **NIRSEG** — singer **(1)**

9. the opposite of sure: **URESUN** — unsure **(1)**

10. in a soft way: **LYFTOS** — softly **(1)**

Theme 4: **Animal Habitats**   43
Assessment Tip: Total **10** Points

Name _____

Prefixes and Suffixes (re-, un-; -ful, -ly, -er)

A **prefix** is a word part added to the beginning of a base word. It adds meaning to the base word.

Prefix		Base Word		New Word	Meaning
re-	+	make	=	**re**make	to make again
un-	+	happy	=	**un**happy	not happy

A **suffix** is a word part added to the end of a base word. It also adds meaning to the base word.

Base Word	Suffix		New Word	Meaning
care	+ -ful	=	care**ful**	full of care
friend	+ -ly	=	friend**ly**	in a friendly way
help	+ -er	=	help**er**	one who helps

Spelling Words

1. helper
2. unfair
3. friendly
4. unhappy
5. remake
6. careful
7. hopeful
8. unlike
9. retell
10. sadly
11. farmer
12. unhurt

Write each Spelling Word under its prefix or suffix.
Order of answers for each category may vary.

re-

remake (**1 point**)

retell (**1**)

un-

unfair (**1**)

unhappy (**1**)

unlike (**1**)

unhurt (**1**)

-ful

careful (**1**)

hopeful (**1**)

-ly

friendly (**1**)

sadly (**1**)

-er

helper (**1**)

farmer (**1**)

Assessment Tip: Total **12** Points

Name _____

Spelling Spree

Base Word Hunt **Write a Spelling Word that has the same base word as each word below.**

1. friendship ___friendly **(1 point)**___

2. sadness ___sadly **(1)**___

3. helpful ___helper **(1)**___

4. likely ___unlike **(1)**___

5. fairness ___unfair **(1)**___

Prefix and Suffix Addition **Write Spelling Words by adding *re-*, *un-*, *-ful*, or *-er* to the words below.**

6. tell ___retell **(1)**___

7. care ___careful **(1)**___

8. happy ___unhappy **(1)**___

9. hope ___hopeful **(1)**___

10. make ___remake **(1)**___

11. hurt ___unhurt **(1)**___

12. farm ___farmer **(1)**___

Spelling Words

1. helper
2. unfair
3. friendly
4. unhappy
5. remake
6. careful
7. hopeful
8. unlike
9. retell
10. sadly
11. farmer
12. unhurt

Theme 4: **Animal Habitats** 45
Assessment Tip: Total **12** Points

Name _____

Proofreading and Writing

Proofreading **Circle the five misspelled Spelling
Words in the report. Then write each word correctly.**

Spelling Words
1. helper
2. unfair
3. friendly
4. unhappy
5. remake
6. careful
7. hopeful
8. unlike
9. retell
10. sadly
11. farmer
12. unhurt

Wildlife Rescue Report

Today I answered a call from a group of friendly
neighbors in the city. Several deer had wandered into a
backyard. The animal control officer arrived, but the
people were (onhappy) about what he proposed to do. I
came with no (helpper,) but I managed to get the deer
onto my truck. The animals were all (unhurte.) A
(farrmer) helped me herd the deer into the woods. I am
(hopful) that they will not wander back to the city again.

1. unhappy **(2 points)**

2. helper **(2)**

3. unhurt **(2)**

4. farmer **(2)**

5. hopeful **(2)**

Write a Letter How would you thank Carl Jackson if
you were Sonia?

**On a separate sheet of paper, write a letter thanking Mr.
Jackson for rescuing the deer. Tell him what you hope
happens to the deer. Use Spelling Words from the list.**

Responses will vary. **(2)**

Assessment Tip: Total **12** Points

Name _____

Which Form Is It?

**Read each sentence. Decide which inflected form of the
base word shown in parentheses belongs in the sentence.
Then write the word in the blank.**

> **easy** *adjective* Needing very little effort; not hard.
> *adjective* **easier, easiest**

> **nod** *verb* To move the head down and then up in a quick motion.
> *noun* A nodding motion.
> *verb* **nodded, nodding**   *noun, plural* **nods**

> **rumble** *verb* To make or move with a deep, long rolling sound.
> *noun* A deep, long rolling sound.
> *verb* **rumbled, rumbling**   *noun, plural* **rumbles**

> **study** *noun* The act or process of learning. 2. A branch of knowledge.
> *verb* **1.** To try to learn. **2.** To examine closely and carefully.
> *noun, plural* **studies**   *verb* **studied, studying**

1. The deer were **(nod)** ___nodding **(2 points)**___
   their heads sleepily.

2. The first truck that **(rumble)** ___rumbled **(2)**___
   down the street was a delivery van.

3. Saving deer is not the **(easy)** ___easiest **(2)**___
   task, but it's worth the effort.

4. Clarence said, "We **(study)** ___studied **(2)**___
   deer in science last year."

5. The wildlife rescuer **(nod)** ___nodded **(2)**___
   in greeting.

6. Sonia felt sad as the truck was **(rumble)** ___rumbling **(2)**___
   away with the deer.

Name _____

Using Irregular Verbs

Complete each sentence with the correct form of the verb in parentheses.

1. One morning, Sonia <u>saw **(1 point)**</u> an amazing sight.
   (see, past)

2. Five deer had <u>come **(1)**</u> into her yard.
   (come, with *had*)

3. The deer <u>ate **(1)**</u> the carrot. (eat, past)

4. The neighbors <u>came **(1)**</u> to see the animals.
   (come, past)

5. Mr. Benny has <u>seen **(1)**</u> deer in the wild.
   (see, with *has*)

6. By morning, the deer had <u>eaten **(1)**</u> a lot of flowers.
   (eat, with *had*)

7. We have <u>done **(1)**</u> everything we can.
   (did, with *have*)

8. The wildlife rescuer <u>went **(1)**</u> to catch the deer.
   (go, past)

9. He <u>did **(1)**</u> his job very well. (do, past)

10. The van with the deer has <u>gone **(1)**</u> to the country.
    (go, with *has*)

Assessment Tip: Total **10** Points

Name _____

Completing Sentences with Irregular Verbs

Complete each sentence with the correct form of the verb in parentheses.

1. The wildlife rescuer <u>gave **(1 point)**</u> the deer medicine to make it tired. (give, past)

2. In a few minutes, the deer <u>grew **(1)**</u> sleepy. (grow, past)

3. The man <u>took **(1)**</u> the deer away from the city. (take, past)

4. The neighbors had <u>taken **(1)**</u> many photographs of the deer. (took, with *had*).

5. The deer have <u>run **(1)**</u> happily in their new home. (run, with *have*)

6. The young deer have <u>grown **(1)**</u> a lot since they were born. (grow, with *have*)

7. A reporter <u>wrote **(1)**</u> about the deer in Sonia's yard. (write, past)

8. He has <u>given **(1)**</u> the story to his editor. (give, with *has*)

9. Sonia <u>ran **(1)**</u> to show the article to her friends. (run, past)

10. She has <u>written **(1)**</u> a poem about the deer. (write, with *has*)

Name _____

Using the Correct Verb Form

Read each sentence. If the verb is correct, write C after the sentence. If the verb is incorrect, rewrite the sentence with the correct form.

1. A squirrel comed into Sonia's house.

   A squirrel **came** into Sonia's house. **(1 point)**

2. It has eated a box of crackers.

   It has **eaten** a box of crackers. **(1)**

3. Sonia runned to tell her parents about the squirrel.

   Sonia **ran** to tell her parents about the squirrel. **(1)**

4. They saw the cracker crumbs in the kitchen.

   C (1)

5. The squirrel had ran out the window.

   The squirrel had **run** out the window. **(1)**

6. They wented to the yard.

   They **went** to the yard. **(1)**

7. The squirrel went up a tree.

   C (1)

8. Sonia has seed the squirrel again.

   Sonia has **seen** the squirrel again. **(1)**

Assessment Tip: Total **8** Points

Name _____

Problem-Solution Planner

Use this page to help you plan a problem-solution essay. Work with a partner. Think of a problem and two ideas to solve it. Tell what happened with each idea. End with a sentence or two that tells how the problem was solved.

Problem:

(2 points)

_____

Solution Idea #1: (2) _____	**Solution Idea #2:** (2) _____
What happened: (2) _____ _____ _____	**What happened:** (2) _____ _____ _____

Problem Solved!

(2)

_____

_____

Name _____

Varying Sentence Types

Writers use the four kinds of sentences to make
their writing more interesting.

► A **statement** tells something and ends with a period:
   Deer live in the woods.

► A **question** asks something and ends with a
   question mark: Do deer live in the woods?

► An **exclamation** shows surprise or another
   strong feeling and ends with an exclamation point:

   Deer visited the city!

► A **command** tells someone to do something and ends
   with a period: Take the deer back to the woods.

**Rewrite each sentence as directed. You may need to
add, remove, or reorder words to change sentence types.**

1. They will think of a way to help the deer.

   Command: ___Think of a way to help the deer. **(2 points)**___

2. Are wild animals safe in the city?

   Exclamation: ___Wild animals aren't safe in the city! **(2)**___

3. Call the animal control officers.

   Statement: ___I (He, She, They, We) will call the animal control officers. **(2)**___

4. What do you see out the window?

   Command: ___Look out the window and tell me what you see. **(2)**___

5. There are four deer in the garden.

   Question: ___Are there four deer in the garden? **(2)**___

Assessment Tip: Total **10** Points

Name _____

Vocabulary Items

Use the test-taking strategies and tips you have learned to help you answer these vocabulary items. This practice will help you when you take this kind of test.

Read each sentence. Choose the word that means about the same as the underlined word. Fill in the circle for the correct answer at the bottom of the page.

1   The sky was <u>speckled</u> with millions of puffins returning to the island.

   (A) spotted

   (B) noisy

   (C) striped

   (D) quiet

2   The birds came to the <u>uninhabited</u> islands to lay their eggs and raise their chicks.

   (F) crowded

   (G) treeless

   (H) dangerous

   (J) deserted

3   The puffins make <u>burrows</u> underground for their nests.

   (A) caves

   (B) tunnels

   (C) hills

   (D) waterways

ANSWER ROWS   1 (A) (B) (C) (D) **(5 points)**   3 (A) ● (C) (D) **(5)**

2 (F) (G) (H) ● **(5)**

Name _____

Vocabulary Items continued

4   The puffins were <u>bobbing</u> up and down on the waves of the sea.

    Ⓕ walking

    Ⓖ bouncing

    Ⓗ sinking

    Ⓙ jumping

5   Arnar <u>spies</u> a puffin flying overhead and tells Halla to look.

    Ⓐ sees

    Ⓑ hides

    Ⓒ catches

    Ⓓ touches

6   Halla and her friends help pufflings that are <u>stranded</u> on land.

    Ⓕ lost

    Ⓖ living

    Ⓗ stuck

    Ⓙ sleeping

ANSWER ROWS   4 Ⓕ **Ⓖ** Ⓗ Ⓙ **(5 points)**   6 Ⓕ Ⓖ **Ⓗ** Ⓙ **(5)**
              5 **Ⓐ** Ⓑ Ⓒ Ⓓ **(5)**

Assessment Tip: Total **30** Points

Name _____

Spelling Review

Write Spelling Words from the list on this page to answer the questions. Order of answers in each category may vary.

1–8. Which eight words have the vowel + *r* sound in *hair*?

1. pear **(1 point)**

2. chair **(1)**

3. scare **(1)**

4. pair **(1)**

5. air **(1)**

6. bare **(1)**

7. care **(1)**

8. bear **(1)**

9–16. Which eight words have endings that have changed the spelling of the base word?

9. parties **(1)**

10. joking **(1)**

11. cared **(1)**

12. babies **(1)**

13. grinning **(1)**

14. chopped **(1)**

15. carried **(1)**

16. smiled **(1)**

17–21. Which five words have the prefix *re-* or *un-*?

17. unhurt **(1)**

18. retell **(1)**

19. unlike **(1)**

20. unhappy **(1)**

21. remake **(1)**

22–25. Which four words have the suffix *-ful*, *-ly*, or *-er*?

22. sadly **(1)**

23. helper **(1)**

24. hopeful **(1)**

25. friendly **(1)**

Spelling Words

1. sadly
2. helper
3. unhurt
4. parties
5. pear
6. retell
7. chair
8. joking
9. unlike
10. scare
11. pair
12. cared
13. babies
14. hopeful
15. air
16. grinning
17. bare
18. chopped
19. care
20. carried
21. friendly
22. bear
23. unhappy
24. remake
25. smiled

Name _____

Spelling Spree

Wacky Rhymes Write a Spelling Word in each sentence that rhymes with the underlined word.

1. air
2. parties
3. grinning
4. pear
5. chair
6. carried
7. babies
8. chopped
9. pair
10. joking
11. unhappy
12. retell

1. I will wear a __pair **(1 point)**__ of new socks to the <u>fair</u>.

2. Who got <u>hair</u> on my good __chair **(1)**__ ?

3. She's __grinning **(1)**__ because our team is <u>winning</u>.

4. They are __joking **(1)**__ and <u>poking</u> at piñatas.

5. When my parents got <u>married</u>, my mother __carried **(1)**__ roses.

Riddle Time Write a Spelling Word to answer each question.

6. What do you blow into a balloon? __air **(1)**__

7. What is a yellow or green fruit that grows on trees? __pear **(1)**__

8. What do you do if you recite a story again? __retell **(1)**__

9. How does somebody wearing a frown feel? __unhappy **(1)**__

10. What has been done to a cut-up apple? __chopped **(1)**__

11. Who are the youngest people? __babies **(1)**__

12. What events can you go to on birthdays? __parties **(1)**__

Assessment Tip: Total **12** Points

Name _____

Proofreading and Writing

Proofreading **Circle the six misspelled Spelling Words in this story. Then write each word correctly.**

Marv, the farm (helpir) worked hard and (caired) for some baby rabbits that were (unliek) others because they were very small. He would (reemake) their beds in his (freindly) way. Marv was (hopefull) they would grow stronger soon.

1. helper **(1 point)**

2. cared **(1)**

3. unlike **(1)**

4. remake **(1)**

5. friendly **(1)**

6. hopeful **(1)**

Spelling Words

1. care
2. friendly
3. smiled
4. unlike
5. sadly
6. scare
7. bare
8. grinning
9. helper
10. cared
11. remake
12. bear
13. hopeful
14. unhurt

Tale of a Bear **Use Spelling Words to complete this story beginning. (1 point each)**

Mimi watched the polar 7. bear **(1)** cub. His

8. bare **(1)** head made her shiver. Mimi looked at the cub

9. sadly **(1)** . Mimi's dad knew that she wanted to take

10. care **(1)** of the cub. He told her it was 11. unhurt **(1)**

by the cold, and icebergs didn't 12. scare **(1)** it. Then Mimi

13. smiled **(1)** happily. She even started 14. grinning **(1)** .

Write a Description **On a separate sheet of paper, write about your favorite animal and where it lives. Use the Spelling Review Words.**
Responses will vary. **(6)**

Name _____

Voyagers

If you were to take a voyage, where would you go? Describe the place and tell why you would go there.
(5 points)

_____

_____

_____

_____

_____

_____

_____

_____

Would you go alone or with other people? What things would you bring with you?
(5)

_____

_____

_____

_____

Assessment Tip: Total **10** Points

Name _____

Voyagers

Fill in the chart as you read the stories. Sample answers shown.

	Across the Wide Dark Sea	Yunmi and Halmoni's Trip	Trapped by the Ice!
Who takes the voyage? **Where does the voyage begin and end?**	Pilgrims travel from England to America. **(2 points)**	Yunmi and her grandmother travel from New York to Korea and back. **(2)**	Shackleton travels from England to Antarctica and back. **(2)**
What qualities help the voyagers succeed?	The Pilgrims are brave, friendly, smart, and hard-working. **(3)**	Yunmi is caring, friendly, responds quickly to change, and learns from her experiences. **(3)**	Shackleton is daring, brave, strong, and good at solving problems. **(3)**

Assessment Tip: Total **15** Points

Name _____

Tale of a Sea Voyage

**On the line after each sentence, write
the correct definition of the underlined word.**

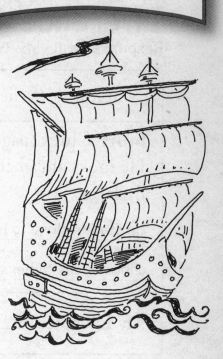

Definitions You Will Need:

► heavy metal object that keeps a ship in place
► crowded
► trip from one place to another
► passing slowly through small openings
► small community in a new place
► stay alive
► tired

1. In 1620, the Pilgrims made a long journey from England to

   America. trip from one place to another **(2 points)** _____

2. With so many people, the ship was cramped. crowded **(2)** _____

3. Water kept seeping through the wooden walls of the ship.

   passing slowly through small openings **(2)** _____

4. When the ship neared land, the crew dropped the anchor.

   heavy metal object that keeps a ship in place **(2)** _____

5. The many hardships made the Pilgrims weary. tired **(2)** _____

6. Even though the voyage was very difficult, all but one of the passengers

   managed to survive. stay alive **(2)** _____

7. After the Pilgrims landed, they chose a spot and built a settlement.

   small community in a new place **(2)** _____

Assessment Tip: Total **14** Points

Name _____

Inference Chart
Responses will vary. Examples are given.

---

1. How does the boy feel when the journey begins?

Story Clues (pages 113–115)	**What I Know**
He looks ahead at the wide dark sea.	Children stay close to their parents
He stands close to his father and	and hold their hands when children
clings to his father's hand. **(1)**	are afraid. **(1 point)**

My Inference The boy is sad and afraid. **(2)**

---

2. How does the boy feel after six weeks at sea?

Story Clues (pages 116–119)	**What I Know**
The ship is crowded, cramped, cold,	It is uncomfortable to be crowded,
and wet. **(1)**	cold, and wet. **(1)**

My Inference He is bored, uncomfortable and worried about the future. **(2)**

---

3. How do the people react to the report of the new land?

Story Clues (pages 122-124)	**What I Know**
The search party finds fine trees,	The materials are good for new
ponds, and rich black earth. **(1)**	homes and growing crops **(1)**

My Inference They are relieved and happy to hear the good news. **(2)**

Name _____

Report on the Journey

Use a complete sentence to answer each question about *Across the Wide Dark Sea*.

1. What are some things the Pilgrims bring with them on the *Mayflower*? They bring tools, goods for trading, guns, food, furniture, clothing, books, and animals. **(1)**

2. Why does the boy tire of being on the ship week after week? There is nothing to do, the food is dull, and the ship is damp, cold, and crowded. **(1)**

3. What serious damage does one storm do to the *Mayflower*? One of the main beams cracks, so the ship begins to leak. **(1)**

4. Why do the people on the *Mayflower* make the dangerous journey? They want to find a place where they can worship God in their own way. **(1)**

5. What do the people fear when they want to go ashore? They fear wild beasts and wild men; they worry that there will be no food, water, or shelter. **(1)**

6. Where do the Pilgrims decide to start their new settlement? They choose a spot high on a hill with a safe harbor, fields, and brooks. **(1)**

7. What are some of the things the Indians teach the Pilgrims? They teach the Pilgrims where to fish and how to plant corn. **(1)**

8. How do the boy and his father feel about the new settlement in the spring? They feel hopeful. **(1)**

Making Good Guesses

**Read the story. Then answer the questions on
the next page.**

A Trip Back in Time!

When Dad said we were going to Plymouth to see where
the Pilgrims lived, Mom looked at us sharply. She said, "I want
you two to behave and learn something today." My sister
Margie smiled and winked at me when Mom looked away.

The place was not at all what we expected. Instead of a
museum display, we found ourselves walking past full-sized
homes with fences and gardens. It looked like New Plymouth
might have looked in 1627. People who dressed and talked like
Pilgrims answered our questions as they went about their tasks
for the day. It seemed as if we had been carried back in time.

The best part of our visit happened by chance. We were
looking at the goats when a young Pilgrim girl came by
with a bucket of water. She told us how the brown goat
had kicked her last week. Then she invited us into her
home, which turned out to be a small, cramped, hot,
smoky cottage with a cooking fire right on the dirt floor.
It was as if we'd made a new friend. We learned all about
Mary, how she did chores most of the day, how she
hated to milk goats, how she loved to
shine the kettle with salt and vinegar.
And she was so polite to all the
adults! Why, she even curtsied to
my parents. Needless to say, we
were too busy talking to get into
trouble — well, on that day anyway!

Making Good Guesses continued

**Use clues from the story and what you know
to answer each question.** Answers will vary. Examples are given.

---

1. What was Margie planning to do?

   She probably was planning to make trouble somehow. **(1 point)**

Story Clues	**What I Know**
She smiled and winked when Mom looked away. **(1)**	Smiling and winking when a parent looks away can mean a secret plan.**(1)**

---

2. How does the storyteller feel about the Pilgrim girl's home?

   She thinks it is small and dirty. **(1)**

Story Clues	**What I Know**
It was small, cramped, hot, and smoky with a cooking fire on the dirt floor. **(1)**	Modern people have bigger homes with stoves and real floors. **(1)**

---

3. What does the storyteller realize about the life of a Pilgrim girl?

   It is very different from her life. **(1)**

Story Clues	**What I Know**
The Pilgrim girl did chores most of the day; she carried water, milked goats, and polished pots; she curtsied. **(2)**	Modern children go to school, play games, and have spare time; they do not curtsy. **(1)**

Name _____

Riddled with Suffixes

**Each word below contains a base word and a suffix.
Write each base word. Put only one letter on each
line. To solve the riddle, write each numbered letter
on the line with the matching number below.**

1. darkness   d(4)   a   r   k   **(1 point)**

2. kindness   k(9)   i   n   d   **(1)**

3. sunless   s   u   n(7)   **(1)**

4. careless   c(5)   a   r   e   **(1)**

5. hopeless   h(6)   o   p(3)   e   **(1)**

6. worthless   w(1)   o   r   t   h   **(1)**

7. goodness   g   o(2)   o   d   **(1)**

8. emptiness   e   m   p   t   y   **(1)**

9. priceless   p   r   i   c(8)   e   **(1)**

10. fearless   f   e   a   r   **(1)**

Native Americans shared more than their food with the
settlers. They also shared their language. Solve the puzzle
to learn one Native American word we use in English.

w(1)   o(2)   o(3)   d(4)   c(5)   h(6)   u(7)   c(8)   k(9)

The Vowel Sounds in
tooth and *cook*

When you hear the /o͞o/ sound, as in *tooth* or *chew*,
remember that it may be spelled with the pattern *oo*
or *ew*. The /o͝o/ sound, as in *cook*, may be spelled with
the pattern *oo*.

/o͞o/ tooth, chew

/o͝o/ cook

▶ In the starred words *shoe* and *blue*, the /o͞o/ sound is
spelled *oe* or *ue*.

Write each Spelling Word under its vowel sound.

Order of answers for each category may vary.

Spelling Words

1. tooth
2. chew
3. grew
4. cook
5. shoe*
6. blue*
7. boot
8. flew
9. shook
10. balloon
11. drew
12. spoon

o͞o

tooth (**1 point**)   boot (**1**)

chew (**1**)   flew (**1**)

grew (**1**)   balloon (**1**)

shoe (**1**)   drew (**1**)

blue (**1**)   spoon (**1**)

o͝o

cook (**1**)   shook (**1**)

Name _____

Spelling Spree

Puzzle Play Write a Spelling Word to fit each clue.

1. a color b **l** u e **(1 point)**

2. a toy you blow up b **a** l l o o n **(1)**

3. not a fork or a knife s p o o **n** **(1)**

4. past tense of *draw* **d** r e w **(1)**

5. a dentist works on it t o o t **h** **(1)**

6. to prepare food by heating c **o** o k **(1)**

Spelling Words

1. tooth
2. chew
3. grew
4. cook
5. shoe*
6. blue*
7. boot
8. flew
9. shook
10. balloon
11. drew
12. spoon

**What two words might someone on a ship be glad to
hear? To find out, write the boxed letters in order.**

l a n d   h o !

**Name Game Write the Spelling Word hidden
in each name. Look for *o*'s and *w*'s to find the
words. Use all small letters in your answers.**

Example: Dr. Diego O. Delgado *good*

7. Mr. Jeb O. Otis   boot **(1)**

8. Miss Peg R. Ewing   grew **(1)**

9. Mrs. Peach E. Wild   chew **(1)**

10. Mr. Cash O. O'Krook   shook **(1)**

Assessment Tip: Total **10** Points

Proofreading and Writing

Proofreading Circle the four misspelled Spelling Words in this diary entry. Then write each word correctly.

> This morning, we had fine sailing weather. Never have I seen a sky so clear and (blew.) Sister and I sat on the deck. We drew pictures of the ship and the sea. Time just (floo) by! Later, the sails (shuk) with a sudden wind, and we were sent below. I lost a (shue) on the stairs as I ran. I will look for it when the storm has passed.

1. tooth
2. chew
3. grew
4. cook
5. shoe*
6. blue*
7. boot
8. flew
9. shook
10. balloon
11. drew
12. spoon

1. blue **(2)**
2. flew **(2)**
3. shook **(2)**
4. shoe **(2)**

Write a Travel Poster The Pilgrims traveled from England to America. Have you taken an interesting trip? Did you travel by ship, car, bus, or plane? What did you see and do?

On a separate sheet of paper, write a travel poster. Make readers want to visit the place you are telling about. Use Spelling Words from the list. Responses will vary. **(2)**

Name _____

Match Words and Syllables

Use the dictionary entries to answer each question below.

desperate *adjective* **1.** Without or nearly without hope.
2. Ready to run any risk because of feeling hopeless.
des•per•ate (dĕs′ pər ĭt) ◊ *adjective*

friend *noun* **1.** A person one knows, likes, and enjoys
being with. **2.** Someone who supports a group, cause, or
movement.
friend (frĕnd) ◊ *noun, plural* **friends**

1. Which word contains one syllable? friend **(2 points)**

2. Which word contains three syllables? desperate **(2)**

3. Which word contains one syllable with two vowels? friend **(2)**

4. What is the first syllable of the word *desperate*? des- **(2)**

5. Show where the word *desperate* can be hyphenated for word breaks.

des-per-ate **(2)**

70   Theme 5: **Voyagers**
Assessment Tip: Total **10** Points

Name _____

Using Pronouns for Nouns

**Circle each subject pronoun in the following paragraph.
Then write each pronoun and the verb it matches on the
lines below the paragraph.**

The anchor rises from the sea. (It) drips water.
Father looks at the ocean. (He) hopes the journey
will be safe. The sailors cheer. (They) want the
journey to begin. (I) hold my mother's hand. (We)
feel nervous and excited.

1. It drips **(1 point)** _____

2. He hopes **(1)** _____

3. They want **(1)** _____

4. I hold **(1)** _____

5. We feel **(1)** _____

Choose the correct verb to complete each sentence.

6. I watch **(1)** _____ the wind in our sail. (watch, watches)

7. It blows **(1)** _____ my hair. (blow, blows)

8. We shout **(1)** _____ to the sailors. (shout, shouts)

9. They answer **(1)** _____ our call. (answer, answers)

10. You hear **(1)** _____ the sound of waves. (hear, hears)

Replacing Nouns with Pronouns

**Rewrite each sentence. Replace each
underlined subject with a subject pronoun.**

1. The ship drops anchor.

   It drops anchor. **(1 point)**

2. Father points to our new home.

   He points to our new home. **(1)**

3. The workers build rough houses.

   They build rough houses. **(1)**

4. Mother nurses the sick.

   She nurses the sick. **(1)**

5. The weather is harsh and dangerous.

   It is harsh and dangerous. **(1)**

6. My brother and I take care of the young children.

   We take care of the young children. **(1)**

7. Mother and Father protect our home.

   They protect our home. **(1)**

8. The fields turn green in May.

   They turn green in May. **(1)**

9. The sun shines across the land.

   It shines across the land. **(1)**

10. Mother, Father, my brother, and I watch the sunrise.

    We watch the sunrise. **(1)**

Assessment Tip: Total **10** Points

Name _____

Combining Sentences with Pronouns

Sentence Combining with Subject Pronouns Combine
each pair of sentences. Use the word in parentheses.

1. You talk to the captain. I talk to the captain. (and)

   You and I talk to the captain. **(1 point)**

2. He watches the ocean. I watch the ocean. (and)

   He and I watch the ocean. **(1)**

3. She helps the sailors. I help the sailors. (and)

   She and I help the sailors. **(1)**

4. They sleep on deck. I sleep on deck. (and)

   They and I sleep on deck. **(1)**

5. You feel the cold wind. They feel the cold wind. (and)

   You and they feel the cold wind. **(1)**

6. He raises the sail. I raise the sail. (and)

   He and I raise the sail. **(1)**

7. He steers the boat. She steers the boat. (or)

   He or she steers the boat. **(1)**

8. You will wake up first. She will wake up first. (or)

   You or she will wake up first. **(1)**

9. He builds the house. She builds the house. (and)

   He and she build the house. **(1)**

10. You plant the corn. I plant the corn. (or)

   You or I plant the corn. **(1)**

Writing a Scene from a Play

Title: The Wide Dark Sea

Scene 1: Time — November 1620

Place — a beach in the new land

Characters

Thomas — a boy about 8 years old

William — his brother, a boy about 6 years old

What Happens in This Scene

The two boys race up and down the beach. They find clams and mussels and eat them raw. They eat too many and then feel sick.

How the Boys Feel

They are happy to be off the ship. They are excited about the beach. They also are glad to eat fresh food like the clams and mussels. When they feel sick, they are sorry they ate too much.

Play-act with a partner and pretend to be one of the two boys. Act out the events under **What Happens in This Scene**. Remember to show how the boys feel about each event.

Make notes on this page for dialogue and action ideas. Then write your scene on another sheet of paper.

Scenes will vary. **(10 points)**

_____

_____

_____

Name _____

Exclamation Points

**Read the play scene. Add exclamation points where
they belong.** (**1 point** for each exclamation point.)

Scene: Place: The Pilgrim settlement on Cape Cod
        Time: A spring day in 1621

Mother: It has been a long, terrible winter. But now it is

spring. Our family has survived. I am so happy.! **(1 point)**

Father: Now the children can go outside and play.

(*The two children run for the door.*) Watch out, Nathan and

Sarah.! You almost knocked over that table. **(1)**

Nathan: (*excitedly*) The sun is shining.! I'll bet it's warm out. **(1)**

Sarah: (*shouting*) Look, Nathan.! There are birds in that tree, **(1)**

and they're making a nest.

Mother: Please calm down, children. Eat your breakfast.

Then you can go out to play.

Father: I am so thankful that we have made it to this new land.! **(1)**

Now write a sentence of your own using an exclamation point.

Responses will vary. **(3)**

_____

_____

_____

Name _____

Revising Your Description

Reread your description. What do you need to make it better? Use this page to help you decide. Put a checkmark in the box for each sentence that describes what you have written.

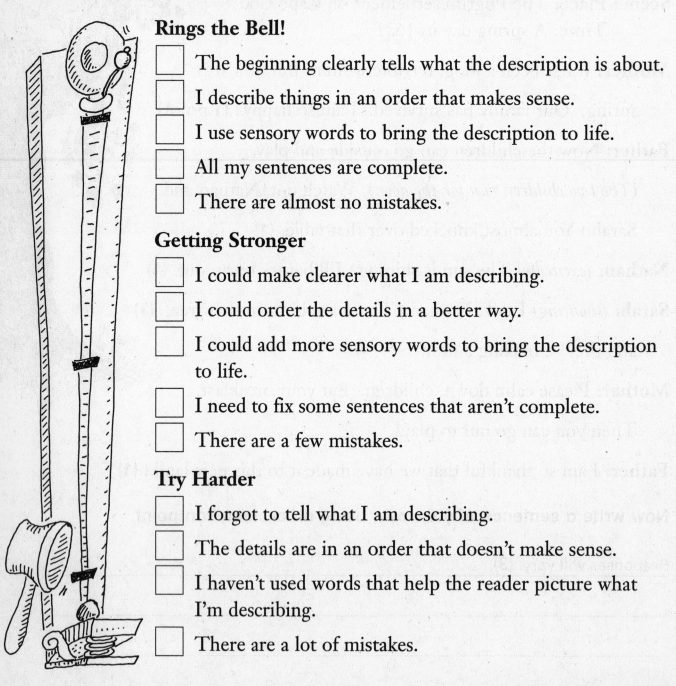

Rings the Bell!

☐ The beginning clearly tells what the description is about.

☐ I describe things in an order that makes sense.

☐ I use sensory words to bring the description to life.

☐ All my sentences are complete.

☐ There are almost no mistakes.

Getting Stronger

☐ I could make clearer what I am describing.

☐ I could order the details in a better way.

☐ I could add more sensory words to bring the description to life.

☐ I need to fix some sentences that aren't complete.

☐ There are a few mistakes.

Try Harder

☐ I forgot to tell what I am describing.

☐ The details are in an order that doesn't make sense.

☐ I haven't used words that help the reader picture what I'm describing.

☐ There are a lot of mistakes.

Name _____

Complete Sentences

Write the words *Complete Sentence* after each complete sentence. Make each incomplete sentence complete by adding words. Answers will vary. Possible responses are provided.

1. San Francisco is America's most hilly town.

   Complete Sentence **(2 points)**

2. Is located right next to the Golden Gate Bridge.

   San Francisco is located right next to the Golden Gate Bridge. **(2)**

3. Some of the hills.

   Some of the hills seem very steep. **(2)**

4. Going down the hills in a car or cable car can seem scary.

   Complete Sentence **(2)**

5. Lombard Street goes back and forth and back and forth.

   Complete Sentence **(2)**

6. Is the crookedest street in the city.

   Lombard Street is the crookedest street in the city. **(2)**

Theme 5: **Voyagers**   77
Assessment Tip: Total **12** Points

Name _____

Spelling Words

Look for spelling patterns you have learned to help you remember the Spelling Words on this page. Think about the parts that you find hard to spell.

Write the missing letters in the Spelling Words below.

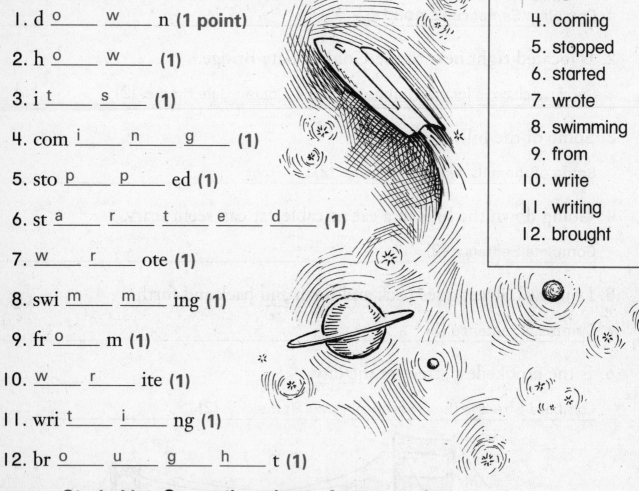

1. d __o__ __w__ n **(1 point)**

2. h __o__ __w__ **(1)**

3. i __t__ __s__ **(1)**

4. com __i__ __n__ __g__ **(1)**

5. sto __p__ __p__ ed **(1)**

6. st __a__ __r__ __t__ __e__ __d__ **(1)**

7. __w__ __r__ ote **(1)**

8. swi __m__ __m__ ing **(1)**

9. fr __o__ m **(1)**

10. __w__ __r__ ite **(1)**

11. wri __t__ __i__ ng **(1)**

12. br __o__ __u__ __g__ __h__ t **(1)**

Spelling Words

1. down
2. how
3. its
4. coming
5. stopped
6. started
7. wrote
8. swimming
9. from
10. write
11. writing
12. brought

✏ **Study List On another sheet of paper, write each Spelling Word. Check the list to be sure you spell each word correctly.** Order of words may vary.

Name _____

Spelling Spree

Find a Rhyme Write a Spelling Word that rhymes with the underlined word.

1. Last <u>night</u> I had to <u>write **(1 point)**</u> a report on Mars.

2. Jamie <u>brought **(1)**</u> home the fish he <u>caught</u>.

3. The statue <u>sits</u> in <u>its **(1)**</u> own room in the museum.

4. Do you know <u>how **(1)**</u> to milk a <u>cow</u>?

5. The teacher <u>wrote **(1)**</u> me a <u>note</u> to give to my parents.

6. These apples <u>come</u> <u>from **(1)**</u> Washington.

7. I sat <u>down **(1)**</u> in my seat just as a <u>clown</u> came on stage.

Spelling Words

1. down
2. how
3. its
4. coming
5. stopped
6. started
7. wrote
8. swimming
9. from
10. write
11. writing
12. brought

Meaning Match Each exercise gives a clue for a word along with an ending. Add the base to the ending to write a Spelling Word. Remember that the spelling of the first word may change.

8. to put words on paper + *ing*
9. to begin + *ed*
10. to move toward the person speaking + *ing*
11. to end + *ed*
12. what you do in a pool + *ing*

8. <u>writing **(1)**</u>
9. <u>started **(1)**</u>
10. <u>coming **(1)**</u>
11. <u>stopped **(1)**</u>
12. <u>swimming **(1)**</u>

Assessment Tip: Total **12** Points

Name _____

Proofreading and Writing

Proofreading Circle the four misspelled Spelling Words in this diary entry. Then write each word correctly.

May 3rd

    Things are going pretty well, except that I'm busy with homework. We have to (rite) a report on an explorer for school. I (startted) writing mine last week. I was going to finish it on Monday, but we went (swiming) instead. Now it's due in two days, and I have to figure out (howe) to finish it on time. I'll be glad when I'm done.

1. down
2. how
3. its
4. coming
5. stopped
6. started
7. wrote
8. swimming
9. from
10. write
11. writing
12. brought

1. write **(2 points)**

2. started **(2)**

3. swimming **(2)**

4. how **(2)**

━━━▶ **Write a Round-Robin Story** Get together in a small group with other students. Then write a story about a voyage, with each of you writing one sentence at a time. Use a Spelling Word from the list in each sentence. Responses will vary. **(2)**

Name _____

Travel Words

Match each word with its definition by writing the letter of the definition on the line beside the word. Then choose a vocabulary word from the list to finish each sentence.

<u>e **(1)**</u> bustling   a. people from outside one's own country

<u>c **(1)**</u> custom   b. person who sells something

<u>a **(1)**</u> foreigners   c. tradition

<u>d **(1)**</u> passport   d. paper allowing someone to visit other countries

<u>f **(1)**</u> sightseeing   e. busy

<u>b **(1)**</u> vendor   f. touring

1. During the summer, many <u>foreigners **(1 point)**</u> visit the United States.

2. Each traveler needs to bring a <u>passport **(1)**</u> in order to enter the country.

3. In New York City, the streets are usually <u>bustling **(1)**</u> with people.

4. Many of the people are tourists going <u>sightseeing **(1)**</u>.

5. On some streets, they can buy hot dogs and other snacks from a <u>vendor **(1)**</u>.

6. In America, it is the <u>custom **(1)**</u> to shake hands with people you meet.

Name _____

Character Chart

Accept varied responses.

Yunmi's Feelings	Story Clues
About Her Visit to Korea excited anxious	*(See page 145.)* from words in the story **(1)** She held Halmoni's hand. **(1)**
About Her Korean Cousins fun to be around **(1 point)** hard to talk to and understand sometimes **(1)** jealous	*(See pages 150–153 and 158–160.)* They take her sightseeing. They show her how to make mandoo. **(1)** Their English is hard to understand and they giggle when she speaks Korean. **(1)** Halmoni pays so much attention to her cousins. **(1)**
About Halmoni misses her attention **(1)** scared, worried, upset **(1)** ashamed about being selfish	*(See pages 152–153 and 157–159.)* Halmoni is busy visiting and overseeing preparations; she gives all her attention to the cousins. **(1)** She sees how happy Halmoni is with her family in Korea. **(1)** from words in the story; she'd be lonely without Halmoni. **(1)**

What do you think Yunmi will do if her cousins come to visit her in New York? Explain why you think as you do.

Accept responses that students can justify. **(2)**

_____

Assessment Tip: Total **14** Points

Name _____

Finish the Letter

Suppose Yunmi wrote this letter. Write story details to finish her letter.

Dear Anna Marie,

　　We've had a wonderful time in Korea! When

<u>Halmoni **(2 points)**</u>　　　　　　　and I first arrived

at the airport, I had to stand in the line for

<u>foreigners **(2)**</u>　　　　　　. That made me feel

strange. However, my Korean family made me feel welcome.

I loved sightseeing and shopping, and my cousins Jinhi and

Sunhi helped me <u>buy a silk purse for you **(2)**</u>. For a

time I became sad, because I thought that my grandmother

<u>wanted to stay in Korea **(2)**</u>. Then we went to my

grandfather's gravesite to <u>celebrate his birthday **(2)**</u>.

That's where Halmoni told me that she would be

<u>coming back to New York **(2)**</u>.

　　Next year I hope that my cousins will come to New York
for a visit. You can help me take them sightseeing! I'll be
home soon, and I can't wait to see you.

　　　　　　　　Your friend,
　　　　　　　　Yunmi

Name _____

Other Outcomes

Read the story. Then complete the chart on the next page.

Ando's Journey

Long ago in Japan, Ando loved to draw. He knew that one day he must follow in his father's footsteps. He must become head firefighter at the castle, as was the custom. But Ando loved to draw.

When Ando was twelve, his mother died. The next year, his father died, so Ando started to work. But he missed drawing so much that he set out to find a teacher. He had to study art.

Ando's first choice was a very famous artist. He begged the artist to help him, but the man simply turned him down, as did many others. Finally, Ando found Toyohiro, a quiet artist who loved nature and made woodblock prints. Ando learned to love nature and make prints much as his teacher did. Ando's work was so beautiful that he helped make this new art style popular.

One day, Ando left for a long journey through Japan. He began drawing everything he saw — mountains, water, the boats in the harbor, people flying kites or drinking tea. Then he turned his pictures into woodblock prints. More than fifty years later, artists in Europe saw a collection of his works. The prints gave them new ideas on drawing and painting.

Name _____

Other Outcomes continued

Answer each question by predicting an outcome.
Then give reasons why you think as you do. Answers will vary.

---

1. What if Ando's parents had not died when he was young?

Predicted Outcome

He might never have become an artist. **(2 points)**

Reasons

His father and mother might have made him follow tradition and become a

firefighter. **(2)**

---

2. What if Ando had never found Toyohiro?

Predicted Outcome

Ando would have kept looking for a teacher until he found one. **(2)**

Reasons

Ando really wanted to become an artist no matter what. I don't give up when

I really want something. **(2)**

**3. What would have been the outcome if Ando had liked to
stay home instead of travel?**

Predicted Outcome

Ando probably would have found other things to draw. **(2)**

Reasons

Ando loved to draw, so he would find something to draw. If I love to do

something, I'll find a way to do it. **(2)**

Name _____

Who Owns It?

▶ Add an **apostrophe** and *s* (*'s*) to a singular noun to make it show ownership. Add an **apostrophe** (*'*) to a plural noun that already ends with *s* to make it show ownership.

Halmoni**'s** hand   parents**'** names

Complete each sentence. Add an apostrophe and *s* or just an apostrophe to make each noun in dark type show ownership. The first one is done for you.

Last weekend, my family went to visit my **(mother)** _mother's_

sister. **(Aunt Jenny)** Aunt Jenny's **(1 point)** _____ house is

three hours away. I carried my two little **(sisters)** sisters' **(1)** _____

bags out to the car. I couldn't lift my **(parents)** parents' **(1)** _____

suitcases because they were too heavy.

I was very excited to see my cousins. My **(cousins)** cousins' **(1)** _____

names are Ryan and Marie. As soon as my family got there, Ryan and

Marie took me to their pet **(rabbits)** rabbits' **(1)** _____ cages

behind the house. **(Ryan)** Ryan's **(1)** _____ rabbit is named

Flopsy. **(Flopsy)** Flopsy's **(1)** _____ ears hang straight down.

(Marie) Marie's **(1)** _____ rabbit is named Topsy. **(Topsy)**

Topsy's **(1)** _____ ears stick straight up.

This time there was a surprise — a rabbit for me! My new **(rabbit)**

rabbit's **(1)** _____ name is Mopsy.

The Vowel Sound in *bought*

When you hear the /ô/ sound, remember that it can be
spelled with the pattern *ough* or *augh*.

/ô/ b**ough**t, c**augh**t

► In the starred words *laugh*, *through*, *enough*, and
cough, the *ough* and *augh* patterns spell other sounds.

**Write each Spelling Word under its *ough* or *augh*
spelling pattern.** Order of answers for each category
may vary.

1. caught
2. thought
3. bought
4. laugh*
5. through*
6. enough*
7. fought
8. daughter
9. taught
10. brought
11. ought
12. cough*

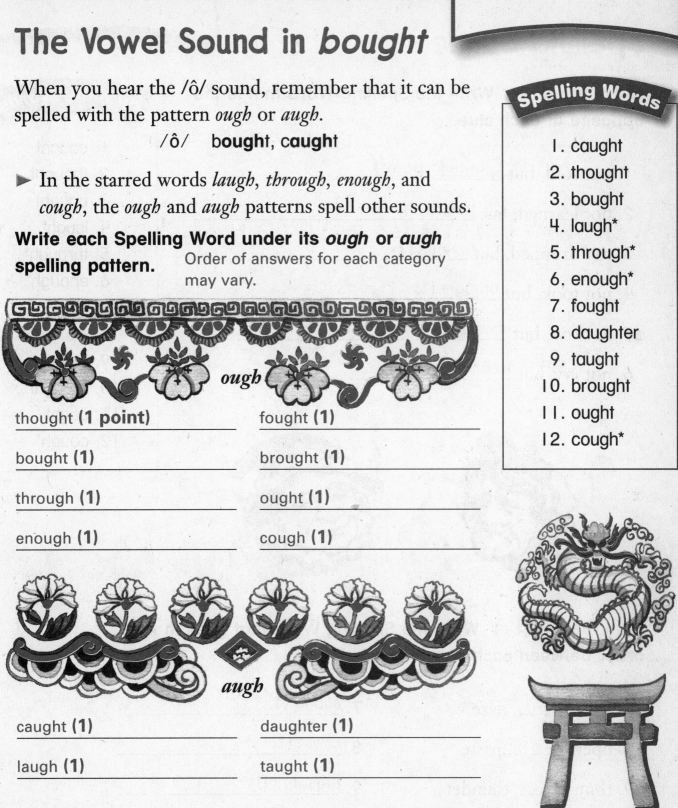

ough

thought **(1 point)**   fought **(1)**

bought **(1)**   brought **(1)**

through **(1)**   ought **(1)**

enough **(1)**   cough **(1)**

augh

caught **(1)**   daughter **(1)**

laugh **(1)**   taught **(1)**

Name _____

Spelling Spree

Only Opposites Write the Spelling Word that is the opposite of each clue.

1. not sold, but <u>bought</u> **(1 point)**

2. not learned, but <u>taught</u> **(1)**

3. not dropped, but <u>caught</u> **(1)**

4. not took, but <u>brought</u> **(1)**

5. not son, but <u>daughter</u> **(1)**

6. not cry, but <u>laugh</u> **(1)**

Alphabet Puzzler Write the Spelling Word that goes in ABC order between each pair of words.

7. cool, _____, daze   7. <u>cough</u> **(1)**

8. open, _____, paste   8. <u>ought</u> **(1)**

9. thin, _____, thunder   9. <u>thought</u> **(1)**

10. find, _____, game   10. <u>fought</u> **(1)**

Assessment Tip: Total **10** Points

Proofreading and Writing

Proofreading **Suppose Yunmi sent this note. Circle the five misspelled Spelling Words in it. Then write each word correctly.**

Dear Mom and Dad,

Halmoni and I are here in Korea! I (thoght) the plane ride was really neat. Everyone loves the presents we brought. We went (throogh) a palace today. I hope we have (enouf) time to see everything. Halmoni has (baught) some gifts for you. You will laugh when you see them!

Your loving (dauter,)

Yunmi

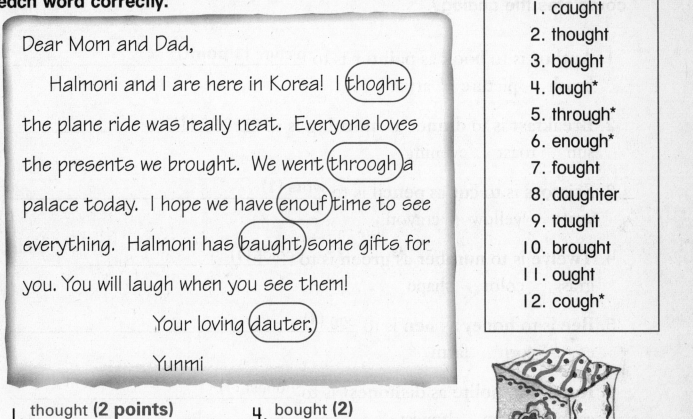

Spelling Words

1. caught
2. thought
3. bought
4. laugh*
5. through*
6. enough*
7. fought
8. daughter
9. taught
10. brought
11. ought
12. cough*

1. thought **(2 points)**
2. through **(2)**
3. enough **(2)**
4. bought **(2)**
5. daughter **(2)**

✏️ **Write an Opinion** An **opinion** tells what you believe or feel about something. Think of two places you have visited. Did you like one place better than the other? Why?

On a separate sheet of paper, write an opinion. Tell about the places you visited, and explain why you liked one place better than the other. Use Spelling Words from the list.

Responses will vary. **(2)**

Name _____

Everything in Its Place

Read the first pair of words in each analogy below. Decide how the words are related. Then write the word that best completes the analogy.

1. **Author** is to **book** as **painter** is to <u>picture **(1 point)**</u> .
   brush   picture   artist

2. **Breakfast** is to **dinner** as **morning** is to <u>evening **(1)**</u> .
   sun   toast   evening

3. **Scissors** is to **cut** as **pencil** is to <u>write **(1)**</u> .
   write   yellow   crayon

4. **Twelve** is to **number** as **green** is to <u>color **(1)**</u> .
   grass   color   shape

5. **Bee** is to **honey** as **hen** is to <u>egg **(1)**</u> .
   egg   corn   farm

6. **Rude** is to **polite** as **dishonest** is to <u>honest **(1)**</u> .
   calm   mean   honest

7. **Television** is to **watch** as **radio** is to <u>listen **(1)**</u> .
   listen   screen   volume

8. **Frog** is to **tadpole** as **butterfly** is to <u>caterpillar **(1)**</u> .
   pretty   caterpillar   flying

Assessment Tip: Total **8** Points

Name _____

Circling Object Pronouns

**Circle each object pronoun in the paragraph below. Then
write the object pronouns on the lines below the paragraph.**

Sunhi shows Yunmi how to make dumplings. She gives (her) a
thin dumpling skin and some filling. Yunmi rolls (it.) She places
the new dumpling on a tray with the other dumplings. The
girls take (them) to the picnic. They share the dumplings with
(us.) Yunmi gives one to (me) to taste.

1. <u>her **(1 point)**</u>   4. <u>us **(1)**</u>

2. <u>it **(1)**</u>   5. <u>me **(1)**</u>

3. <u>them **(1)**</u>

**Choose the correct word or phrase
in parentheses to complete
each sentence.**

6. The picnic is a special event for
<u>us **(1)**</u>. (we, us)

7. Yunmi tells <u>them **(1)**</u> about life in New York. (they, them)

8. Halmoni tells <u>her **(1)**</u> a story. (her, she)

9. Her voice makes <u>me **(1)**</u> feel better. (me, I)

10. The picnic made <u>Halmoni and me **(1)**</u> very
happy. (me and Halmoni, Halmoni and me)

Name _____

Rewriting with Object Pronouns

Object Pronouns	
Singular	**Plural**
me you him, her, it	us you them

Rewrite each sentence. Replace each underlined word or phrase with an object pronoun.

1. The airplane takes <u>Halmoni and Yunmi</u> to Korea.

   The airplane takes them to Korea. **(2 points)**

2. Yunmi shows her passport to <u>the man</u>.

   Yunmi shows her passport to him. **(2)**

3. Outside the airport, Yunmi hugs <u>her cousins</u>.

   Outside the airport, Yunmi hugs them. **(2)**

4. Yunmi buys <u>the purse</u> for <u>Helen</u>.

   Yunmi buys it for her. **(2)**

5. Halmoni takes <u>Yunmi and her cousins</u> to the National Museum.

   Halmoni takes them to the National Museum. **(2)**

Assessment Tip: Total **10** Points

Name _____

Using the Correct Pronoun

What if Yunmi sent her friend this postcard? Circle any pronouns that are used incorrectly. Then rewrite the postcard. (1 point for each)

Dear Helen,

Korea is wonderful. (Halmoni and me) arrived last week. (Her) showed me many wonderful sights. (Us) went to the National Museum with my cousins, Sunhi and Jinhi. (Them) took us to a market too. One vendor sold bean cakes. Sunhi and I picked out this card.

Halmoni showed (I and Sunhi) how to make dumplings. I will be home soon. (Me and you) will make some dumplings!

Bye,
Yunmi

Dear Helen,

Korea is wonderful. Halmoni and **I** arrived last week. **She** showed me many wonderful sights. **We** went to the National Museum with my cousins, Sunhi and Jinhi. **They** took us to a market too. One vendor sold bean cakes. Sunhi and I picked out this card.

Halmoni showed **Sunhi and me** how to make dumplings. I will be home soon. **You and I** will make some dumplings!

Bye,

Yunmi

Name _____

Writing a Message

Use this page to take a message.

Date: _____ **(1 point)** Time: _____ **(1)**

For: _____ **(1)**

From: _____ **(1)** Telephone number: _____ **(1)**

Message: _____ **(4)**

_____

_____

_____

_____

_____

_____

Message taken by: _____ **(1)**

94   Theme 5: **Voyagers**
Assessment Tip: Total **10** Points

Using Complete Information

**Suppose Yunmi and Halmoni each made a phone call. "Listen" to each
answering machine and read the message. Make the messages
complete by adding any missing information.**

1. Hi, Halmoni, it's Yunmi. It's 3:00 on Monday. Junhi and I are going to the park. We will be home at 5:30. If you need us, you can call Mr. Choi's market at 333-6748. He will get the message to us.

Day: Monday. **Time:** 3:00 **(1 point)**
For: Halmoni
Caller: Yunmi **(1)**
Caller's number: 333-6748 **(1)**
Message: Junhi and I are going to the park **(1)** . We will be home at 5:30 **(1)** . Call Mr. Choi's market if you need us.

2. Hello, Junhi and Sunhi. This is Halmoni, on Tuesday at 11:30. I want you to teach Yunmi how to make mandoo on Wednesday afternoon. I'll be home to help you. Leave a message for me at 333-2135.

Day: Tuesday **(1)** **Time:** 11:30
For: Junhi and Sunhi **(1)**
Caller: Halmoni
Caller's number: 333-2135
Message: Teach Yunmi how to make mandoo on Wednesday afternoon. **(2)** I'll be home to help you. Leave a message for me at 333-2135 **(1)** .

Name _____

Selection Vocabulary

Cross out the word that doesn't belong.

1. terrain   earth   ~~sky~~   land   **(1 point)**

2. grueling   ~~resting~~   tiring   difficult   **(1)**

3. perilous   dangerous   ~~safe~~   risky   **(1)**

4. deserted   empty   uninhabited   ~~bustling~~   **(1)**

True or False?

5. It is easy to walk across something <u>impassable</u>.

   false **(1)**

6. Ice sheets floating on water are called <u>floes</u>.

   true **(1)**

7. Land that is <u>barren</u> has many plants and animals.

   false **(1)**

8. A <u>crevasse</u> is a deep crack.

   true **(1)**

Name _____

Text Organization Chart

Text Feature	Where It Is	Purpose
heading (date)	pp. 172, 174, 176, 180, 182, 184, 186, 190, 192, 196, 198 **(1 point)**	helps readers follow the order of events **(1)**
photograph, caption, illustration	pp. 172–179 **(1)**	helps readers understand the text; gives more details **(1)**
definition	p. 190 "Graybeards are monstrous waves that come quietly and quickly, threatening everything in their path." **(1)**	helps readers understand the meaning of a special term **(1)**
chronological sequence	Page 172: The first event takes place on October 27, 1915. Page 198: The last event takes place on May 20, 1916. **(1)**	helps readers understand the order of events **(1)**

Name _____

Shackleton Survives!

**Complete the news report by
adding the missing information.**

Sir Ernest Shackleton and his crew survived many hardships on

their recent voyage to <u>Antarctica **(1)**</u>. Hundreds

of miles from land, their ship, the <u>Endurance **(1 point)**</u>,

became <u>trapped in ice **(1)**</u>. The men camped for

months on slowly moving <u>ice floes **(1)**</u>. When they

reached open water, they set out in lifeboats on a perilous voyage to

<u>Elephant Island **(1)**</u>.

There, the men split up. Shackleton and five others sailed on

toward <u>South Georgia Island **(1)**</u>. The

six men finally landed. Shackleton and two others hiked across tall

<u>mountains **(1)**</u> to get to a <u>whaling station **(1)**</u>,

where they hoped to find <u>people who could help them **(1)**</u>.

On May 20, 1916, the three exhausted men reached safety, but the

voyage did not really end until more than three months later, when

Shackleton <u>rescued all the crew members who had</u>

<u>been left behind. **(1)**</u>.

Assessment Tip: Total **10** Points

Name _____

Organized Hike

Read this news story. Then complete the chart on the next page.

Hiker Stranded

Lost

7:00 P.M. on April 1: Donald McCarthy, 53, of Keene, New Hampshire, got lost while hiking along an old logging trail near Waterville Valley. (A logging trail is used by workers who take away cut trees.) By nightfall, McCarthy knew he would have to spend the night in the woods.

. . . and Found

8:00 P.M.: A Fish and Game officer thought he spotted McCarthy and called out. McCarthy never answered, and the officer moved on. The next morning, McCarthy was found. When questioned by Fish and Game, McCarthy admitted he thought he heard someone call, but he also heard noises in the brush. "I was sure it was a bear," McCarthy said, "so I kept quiet and climbed into a tree for the night."

Bear Sighted in Area: Use Caution

This sign led McCarthy into thinking he heard bears.

Name _____

Organized Hike   continued

Finish the chart with text features from "Hiker Stranded." Explain the purpose of each feature.

Example of Text Feature	Purpose of the Text Feature
Heading Lost; . . . and Found **(1 point)**	to help readers follow the order of events **(1)**
Caption This sign led McCarthy into thinking he heard bears. **(1)**	to give more details about the text **(1)**
Definition A logging trail is used by workers who take away cut trees. **(1)**	to help explain the special term **(1)**
Chronological sequence (dates, times) 7 P.M., April 1; 8 P.M. **(1)**	to help explain the order of events **(1)**

If you were a reporter, what other information would you add?
What text feature would you use to give more information?

Answers will vary. **(2)**

_____

Assessment Tip: Total **10** Points

VCCV Challenge

Write the VCCV word that matches each clue in the puzzle.
Use the Word Bank and a dictionary for help.

Across

1. soaking wet **(1 point)**
6. wood used for building **(1)**
7. the coldest season **(1)**
8. captain of a ship **(1)**
9. to save from danger **(1)**

Down

1. the peak of a mountain **(1)**
2. cloth used for making tents or sails **(1)**
3. an Antarctic bird **(1)**
4. a long trip **(1)**
5. to remain alive **(1)**

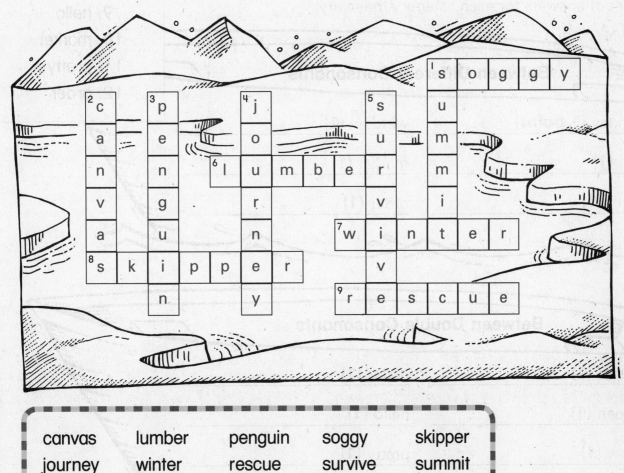

| canvas | lumber | penguin | soggy | skipper |
| journey | winter | rescue | survive | summit |

Assessment Tip: Total **10** Points

Name _____

The VCCV Pattern

To spell a word with the VCCV pattern, divide the word between the two consonants. Look for spelling patterns you have learned. Spell the word by syllables.

vc|cv  vc|cv

Mon | day   sud | den

Spelling Words

1. Monday
2. sudden
3. until
4. forget
5. happen
6. follow
7. dollar
8. window
9. hello
10. market
11. pretty
12. order

Write each Spelling Word under the head that tells where the word is divided into syllables.

Order of answers for each category may vary.

Between Different Consonants

Monday **(1 point)**   window **(1)**

until **(1)**   market **(1)**

forget **(1)**   order **(1)**

Between Double Consonants

sudden **(1)**   dollar **(1)**

happen **(1)**   hello **(1)**

follow **(1)**   pretty **(1)**

Assessment Tip: Total **12** Points

Name _____

Spelling Spree

Silly Statements Each statement was made by a
South Pole visitor. Write the Spelling Word that best
completes each sentence.

1. I will not sell my mittens for a _____.

2. I won't go home _____ I've seen a whale.

3. A seal just tried to climb through my _____.

4. I said _____ to the iceberg as it passed.

5. Please run to the _____ to buy some oranges.

6. That polar bear keeps trying to _____ me around.

7. The little bird in the tux will take your _____.

1. Monday
2. sudden
3. until
4. forget
5. happen
6. follow
7. dollar
8. window
9. hello
10. market
11. pretty
12. order

1. dollar **(2 points)** _____

2. until **(2)** _____

3. window **(2)** _____

4. hello **(2)** _____

5. market **(2)** _____

6. follow **(2)** _____

7. order **(2)** _____

Theme 5: **Voyagers**   103
Assessment Tip: Total **14** Points

Name _____

Proofreading and Writing

Proofreading Circle the five misspelled Spelling Words in this script. Then write each word correctly.

Sam:	We are leaving (Mondy) for a trip to the South Pole.
Emma:	Wow! I didn't know that. Is this a (suddin) trip?
Sam:	No, we've been planning it for ages. I hear it's a really (pritty) place.
Emma:	If you (hapen) to see any penguins, say hello for me.
Sam:	Sure. If you want me to say hi to a killer whale, though, you can (ferget) it!

Spelling Words

1. Monday
2. sudden
3. until
4. forget
5. happen
6. follow
7. dollar
8. window
9. hello
10. market
11. pretty
12. order

1. Monday **(2 points)**

2. sudden **(2)**

3. pretty **(2)**

4. happen **(2)**

5. forget **(2)**

Write a List How would you prepare for a trip to the South Pole? Would you need to buy things? If so, what? Where would you buy the goods?

On a separate sheet of paper, write a list of things to do to get ready for a trip to the South Pole. Use Spelling Words from the list. Responses will vary. **(2)**

Name _____

Sounds the Same

From the word box below, choose a pair of homophones to complete each pair of sentences. Choose the spelling that fits the meaning of the sentence and write it in the blank. Use a dictionary if you are not sure which is which.

not	one	see	threw	bear
knot	won	sea	through	bare

1. a. I stood on the ship's deck and looked out at the

   __sea__ **(1 point)** .

   b. I could __see (1)__ nothing but water and sky.

2. a. Jen __threw (1)__ the ball.

   b. It went __through (1)__ the hoop!

3. a. There was a __knot (1)__ in Jeb's shoelace.

   b. He could __not (1)__ untie it.

4. a. The __bare (1)__ ground was now covered with

   snow.

   b. The big __bear (1)__ left tracks where he walked.

5. a. Our team has only __one (1)__ good pitcher.

   b. Even so, we have __won (1)__ every game.

Name _____

Writing Possessively

Write the possessive pronoun in each sentence.

1. The men began their voyage in 1915. _their_ **(1 point)**

2. Shackleton and his crew were very brave. _his_ **(1)**

3. Our class read about the amazing adventure. _our_ **(1)**

4. I asked my teacher about ice floes. _my_ **(1)**

5. Her explanation was clear and helpful. _her_ **(1)**

Write the possessive pronoun that could take the place of the underlined word or words.

6. I think that <u>Shackleton's</u> story is remarkable. _his_ **(1)**

7. I admire <u>the men's</u> courage. _their_ **(1)**

8. <u>The station's</u> light was a marvelous sight. _Its_ **(1)**

9. Shackleton returned to <u>John, Chippy, and Tim's</u> camp.

   their **(1)**

10. Thoralf was happy to see <u>Thoralf's</u> old friend.

    his **(1)**

Name _____

Choosing Possessives

Choose the correct word in parentheses to complete each sentence.

1. Shackleton led ___his **(1 point)**___ crew to Antarctica. (him, his)

2. The *Endurance* was a useless hulk, lying on ___its **(1)**___ side. (it's, its)

3. The men carried ___their **(1)**___ food with them. (they, their)

4. ___Their **(1)**___ journey was just beginning. (Their, There)

5. Shackleton described ___his **(1)**___ plan. (he's, his)

6. The lifeboats were ___their **(1)**___ only hope. (their, they're)

7. Each boat had ___its **(1)**___ own sled. (its, its')

8. ___Our **(1)**___ class studied the perilous trip. (Our, Ours)

9. I decided to write ___my **(1)**___ story about Antarctica. (me, my)

10. Is ___your **(1)**___ story about Shackleton? (your, you)

Name _____

Writing a Story

Alana wrote a story about Shackleton's crew. Proofread Alana's writing. Check that *its* and *it's* are used correctly. Then rewrite the letter on the lines below. (1 point each)

> May 19, 1916
>
> Its very cold again today. John and Chippy are still very ill. The sun is bright, but it's light brings no heat. This barren land is deserted and lonely.
>
> I explored the terrain yesterday. Its difficult to follow a trail. At last, I killed a seal. It's meat will feed us for several days. The food is so cold it has lost it's taste.
>
> I hope that Shackleton and the others can survive their journey. Its hard to imagine a more grueling adventure.

May 19, 1916

It's very cold again today. John and Chippy are still very ill. The

sunis bright, but **its** light brings no heat. This barren land is deserted

and lonely.

I explored the terrain yesterday. **It's** difficult to follow a trail.

At last, I killed a seal. **Its** meat will feed us for several days. The food

is so cold it has lost **its** taste.

I hope that Shackleton and the others can survive their perilous

journey. **It's** hard to imagine a more grueling adventure.

Assessment Tip: Total **6** Points

Name _____

A Learning Log Entry

Pick two examples of your own writing. Carefully reread your work. Complete the Learning Log entry. List what you have learned under *What I Learned*. List what needs more work under *My Goals*.

<table>
<tr><td colspan="2" align="center">**LEARNING LOG**</td></tr>
<tr><td>Writing sample 1: _____</td><td>Date: _____</td></tr>
<tr><td>Writing sample 2: _____</td><td>Date: _____</td></tr>
</table>

What I Learned:	**My Goals:**
(5 points)	**(5)**
_____	_____
_____	_____
_____	_____
_____	_____
_____	_____
_____	_____

Name _____

Using Dates and Times

► Dates are written: Month, day, year. A comma separates the
day and year. Dates can also be written in numerals with
slash marks.

  The fifth of February in 2003: February 5, 2003
    or 2/5/03

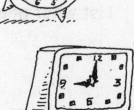

► A.M. stands for morning, from one minute after
midnight until noon. Seven o'clock in the morning: 7:00 A.M.

► P.M. stands for after noon, from one minute after
noon until midnight. Nine o'clock in the evening: 9:00 P.M.

Write each date two ways.

1. The seventh day of April in 2011

   April 7, 2011 **(1 point)**   4/7/11 **(1)**

2. The thirty-first of October in 2006

   October 31, 2006 **(1)**   10/31/06 **(1)**

Write each time.

3. Six-fifteen
   (after noon)

   6:15 P.M. **(1)**

4. Eight thirty-five
   (morning)

   8:35 A.M. **(1)**

5. Ten minutes after ten
   (morning)

   10:10 A.M. **(1)**

6. Forty minutes after nine
   (after noon)

   9:40 P.M. **(1)**

Assessment Tip: Total **8** Points

Name _____

Writing an Answer to a Question

Use what you have learned about taking tests to help you write answers to questions about something you have read. This practice will help you when you take this kind of test.

Read these paragraphs from the story *Yunmi and Halmoni's Trip*.

>   Yunmi had only been to a cemetery once before. She had seen people place flowers at a grave, say a prayer, and leave quietly. But in Korea, no one cried or looked sad. The cousins ran through the field collecting flowers and smooth stones for Grandfather's hill.
>   Yunmi wanted to talk with Halmoni, but everyone was crowded around her. Yunmi went and sat under a big tree all by herself to think. As she watched Halmoni, Yunmi grew more and more afraid that Halmoni would not want to go back to New York.

Now write your answer to each question.

1. How do you think Yunmi's life would change if her grandmother, Halmoni, did not go back to New York with her?
   (predicting outcomes)

   Sample answer: Yunmi would not be able to do things with her

   grandmother. She would probably not be as close to her grandmother,

   and she would not see her grandmother very often because Korea is far

   from New York. **(5 points)**

Assessment Tip: Total **5** Points

Name _____

Writing an Answer to a Question continued

2. What does Yunmi do when she worries about going back to New York without her grandmother? *(cause and effect)*

   Sample answer: Yunmi tries to talk to Halmoni but can't because the

   others are crowded around her grandmother. Yunmi sits under a

   tree by herself. **(5)**

   _____

   _____

3. How do people in Korea act when they visit a grave in a cemetery? *(making generalizations)*

   Sample answer: No one looks sad or cries. People collect stones

   and flowers for the grave. **(5)**

   _____

   _____

Name _____

Spelling Review

Write Spelling Words from the list on this page to answer the questions. Order of answers in each category may vary.

1–8. Which eight words have the vowel sound in **loose** or **look**?

1. grew **(1 point)**

2. flew **(1)**

3. spoon **(1)**

4. cook **(1)**

5. boot **(1)**

6. balloon **(1)**

7. chew **(1)**

8. tooth **(1)**

9–15. Which seven words have the vowel sound in **fought**?

9. bought **(1)**

10. caught **(1)**

11. thought **(1)**

12. daughter **(1)**

13. brought **(1)**

14. ought **(1)**

15. taught **(1)**

16–26. Which eleven words have the VCCV pattern?
Hint: You have already written one of these words.

16. order **(1)**

17. hello **(1)**

18. happen **(1)**

19. forget **(1)**

20. window **(1)**

21. dollar **(1)**

22. Monday **(1)**

23. sudden **(1)**

24. pretty **(1)**

25. until **(1)**

26. balloon **(1)**

Spelling Words

1. bought
2. order
3. grew
4. hello
5. thought
6. happen
7. forget
8. caught
9. flew
10. spoon
11. daughter
12. window
13. dollar
14. brought
15. cook
16. boot
17. Monday
18. sudden
19. pretty
20. until
21. ought
22. balloon
23. chew
24. taught
25. tooth

Assessment Tip: Total **26** Points

Name _____

Spelling Spree

New TV Shows! Write the Spelling Word that best completes each title of a new TV show. Remember to use capital letters.

1. *Sook Can _____, Bake, and Roast*
2. *Look Out the _____. What Do You See?*
3. *The Superhero Who _____ Too High*
4. *Alphabetical _____: A Game Show for the Very Young*
5. *I _____ to Have Brought My Camera*
6. *A _____ Storm Springs Up in Egypt*
7. *Always _____ Your Food Well*
8. *Tongue, _____, and Throat: Have a Healthy Mouth*

1. brought
2. cook
3. until
4. flew
5. tooth
6. chew
7. happen
8. ought
9. boot
10. sudden
11. order
12. spoon
13. window
14. Monday

1. <u>Cook</u> **(1 point)**
2. <u>Window</u> **(1)**
3. <u>Flew</u> **(1)**
4. <u>Order</u> **(1)**
5. <u>Ought</u> **(1)**
6. <u>Sudden</u> **(1)**
7. <u>Chew</u> **(1)**
8. <u>Tooth</u> **(1)**

A Strange Hike A few words are missing from this paragraph. Use a Spelling Word to fill in each blank.

We went hiking on 9. <u>Monday</u> **(1)**. It had to

10. <u>happen</u> **(1)** that the laces on my left

11. <u>boot</u> **(1)** broke. Then we found out that no

one had 12. <u>brought</u> **(1)** any food. However, we did

find one plastic 13. <u>spoon</u> **(1)**. The weather was warm

14. <u>until</u> **(1)** the afternoon. That's when we went home.

Assessment Tip: Total **14** Points

Proofreading and Writing

Proofreading Circle the five misspelled Spelling Words below. Then write each word correctly.

I flew in a hot-air (baloon!) My uncle (bot) it from his friend. I never (thoght) it could go so high. The city looked (pritty) from up high. I will never (fourget) the ride.

Spelling Words

1. balloon
2. thought
3. grew
4. caught
5. forget
6. bought
7. pretty
8. dollar
9. until
10. taught
11. daughter
12. hello

1. balloon **(1 point)**
2. bought **(1)**
3. thought **(1)**
4. pretty **(1)**
5. forget **(1)**

Today's News Fix this speech. Write the Spelling Word that is the opposite of each underlined word.

Who 6. <u>learned</u> that we all should travel by car? Last year, the number of cars 7. <u>shrank</u>. Even my 8. <u>son</u> has her own car. Say good-bye to cars and 9. <u>good-bye</u> to trains! People have 10. <u>let go</u> of the excitement of train travel. If everyone gave one 11. <u>coin</u>, we could have a train tomorrow, but 12. <u>after</u> then, we won't!

6. taught **(1)**
7. grew **(1)**
8. daughter **(1)**
9. hello **(1)**
10. caught **(1)**
11. dollar **(1)**
12. until **(1)**

✏➤ **Write a Story** On another sheet of paper, write about a trip you would like to take. Use the Spelling Review Words. Responses will vary. **(3)**

Name _____

Best Beginnings

Write a shorter version of the opening sentences of each biography. Then describe which opening most made you want to read the rest of the biography.

Becoming a Champion: The Babe Didrikson Story

(2 points) _____

_____

Bill Meléndez: An Artist in Motion

(2) _____

_____

Brave Bessie Coleman: Pioneer Aviator

(2) _____

_____

Hank Greenberg: All-Around All-Star

(2) _____

_____

Which opening made you want to read the biography?

(2) _____

How might reading this biography change your life?

(2) _____

_____

Name _____

When They Were Young

Write one fact about each person's childhood. Tell how that fact affected each person as an adult.

Babe Didrikson

(2 points)

_____

_____

Bill Meléndez

(2)

_____

_____

Bessie Coleman

(2)

_____

_____

Hank Greenberg

(2)

_____

_____

What is something you can do as a young person that will help you when you are grown-up?

(2)

_____

_____

Assessment Tip: Total **10** Points

Name _____

Smart Solutions

Describe a problem that you would like to solve.
Tell why you think it is important to solve it.

(5 points)

_____

_____

_____

_____

_____

_____

_____

_____

What could you do to help solve this problem?

(5) _____

_____

_____

_____

_____

Name _____

Smart Solutions

Fill in the chart as you read the stories.

Sample answers shown.

	Pepita Talks Twice	**Poppa's New Pants**	**Ramona Quimby, Age 8**
What is the problem?	Pepita doesn't want to speak twice all the time. She wants more time to play with her dog, Lobo. **(2 points)**	Poppa needs his new pants to be hemmed. **(2)**	The Quimbys are crabby because they are stuck inside the house on a rainy Sunday. **(2)**
How is the problem solved?	Not speaking Spanish creates more problems, so Pepita decides it is good to speak two languages. **(3 points)**	Poppa's family makes his pants too short, so they give them to George. **(3)**	The Quimbys go out for dinner, have a nice meal, and learn to enjoy being together again. **(3)**

Assessment Tip: Total **15** Points

Name _____

Create a Crossword!

Use the words in the box to create your own crossword
puzzle. On another sheet of paper, write a clue for each
word you use. (**2 points** for using word and writing an appropriate clue)

Sample puzzle is given.

Vocabulary

enchiladas	language	Spanish	salsa
tacos	tamales	tortilla	

	¹L				²S						
	A				P		³S				
⁴E	N	C	H	I	L	A	D	A	S		
	G				A		A				
	U		⁵T		N		L				
⁶T	A	C	O	S		I	S	A			
	G		R		S	H					
	E		T								
			I								
			L								
			L								
	⁷T	A	M	A	L	E	S				

Name _____

Problem-Solving Chart

Problem: Pepita does not like having to talk twice.	

Responses may vary.

Possible Solutions	Pros (+) and Cons (−)
1. Stop speaking Spanish.	(+) You wouldn't have to talk twice for people anymore. (−) You wouldn't be able to talk with people who spoke only Spanish. **(2 points)**
2. Stop speaking English.	(+) You wouldn't have to talk twice for people anymore. **(2)** (−) You wouldn't be able to talk with people who spoke only English. **(2)**
3. Get mad and point out that you don't have time to speak twice.	(+) People would stop asking you to talk twice. **(2)** (−) You would probably lose a lot of friends. **(2)**
4. Politely say that you can't speak twice when you don't have time.	(+) Most people would probably stop asking you to talk twice. **(2)** (+) You could still talk with people who speak only Spanish or English. **(2)**

Assessment Tip: Total **14** Points

Name _____

What Happened?

Mark a T if the sentence is true and an F if it is false.
If the sentence is false, rewrite it to make it correct.

1. Pepita's dog is a wolf.

   F Pepita's dog is named Lobo, which means wolf. **(1 point)**

2. Some adults in Pepita's neighborhood speak only Spanish.

   T **(1)**

3. Pepita loses her temper when Juan gets home first and teaches Lobo to fetch a ball.

   T **(1)**

4. Before she makes her decision, Pepita thinks about all the problems she might have if she stops speaking Spanish.

   F Pepita does not think about the problems she might have. **(1)**

5. Lobo does not understand Pepita when she speaks in English.

   T **(1)**

6. Pepita's father is happy when he learns that Pepita has stopped speaking Spanish.

   F Pepita's father is upset. **(1)**

Write a complete sentence to answer the question below.

What event finally convinces Pepita that it is a good thing to speak both English and Spanish?

She saves Lobo from getting hit when she calls to him in Spanish. **(2)**

Name _____

A Homework Problem

Read the story. Then complete the chart on the next page.

The Volcano or Numberland

"Pakki! Help me in the kitchen! Now! Hurry!" I ran down to the kitchen, terrified. There sat my sister, Kayla, drinking milk and calmly reading the television listings in the newspaper.

"What's wrong?" I asked, out of breath from running to the kitchen.

"The science project I've been working on for two weeks is due tomorrow. Ms. Odenpak may give me a bad grade if I don't have my model volcano finished. But a TV show called *Niles in Numberland* is starting in twenty minutes. My math teacher, Mr. Browning, told us to watch it and be ready to talk about it tomorrow in class. What I should do? Help!"

"I have three ideas," I answered. "One, you finish your volcano while I watch the TV show and take notes. Of course, I'm not very good at taking notes," I reminded her. "Two, you can watch the TV show and ask Ms. Odenpak for an extra day to finish your volcano. Or three, you can work on your volcano in front of the television while you take notes on the show."

"Hmm," Kayla answered, thinking deeply. "Which one's the best solution?"

Name _____

A Homework Problem continued

Read the problem. Write one possible solution from the story in each box. Then give a pro and a con about the solution.

The Problem: Kayla needs to finish her science project, and she also needs to watch TV for a math assignment.

Possible Solution: Kayla can finish the volcano while Pakki takes notes on the TV show. **(1 point)**

Pro: Kayla will be able to finish both assignments on time. **(1)**

Con: Pakki's notes might not be good enough for the discussion. **(1)**

Possible Solution: Kayla can watch the TV show and ask Ms. Odenpak for an extra day to finish her volcano. **(1)**

Pro: Kayla will take her own notes and be prepared to talk. **(1)**

Con: If she doesn't get an extra day, she might fail. **(1)**

Possible Solution: Kayla can finish the volcano in front of the television while she's taking notes on the TV show. **(1)**

Pro: Kayla will be able to finish both assignments on time. **(1)**

Con: Her attention will be split, so she may not do either well. **(1)**

Which of these solutions do you think is the best? Why? Answers will vary.

The last solution seems best because she'll finish both. **(1)**

Theme 6: **Smart Solutions**   125
Assessment Tip: Total **10** Points

Name _____

Playing with the Pattern

Read each word in dark type. Then follow the directions to make a new word. Write the new word on the line, and draw a picture in the box to show its meaning.

Example: **single**   Replace **si** with **ju**.

The new word is _____jungle_____.

1. **bundle**   Replace **bu** with **ca**.

   The new word is _candle_ **(1 point)**___.

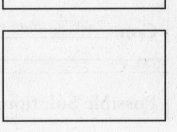

2. **dollar**   Replace **lar** with **phin**.

   The new word is _dolphin_ **(1)**___.

3. **twinkle**   Replace **twi** with **a**.

   The new word is _ankle_ **(1)**___.

4. **letter**   Replace **let** with **mons**.

   The new word is _monster_ **(1)**___.

5. **turtle**   Replace **tur** with **cas**.

   The new word is _castle_ **(1)**___.

(1 point for each picture**)**

Words That End with *er* or *le*

Remember that, in words with more than one syllable, the final /ər/ sounds are often spelled *er*; and the final /əl/ sounds can be spelled *le*.

/ər/ summ**er**　　/əl/ litt**le**

► In the starred word *travel*, the /əl/ sound is spelled *el*.
► In the starred word *color*, the /ər/ sound is spelled *or*.

Write each Spelling Word under the heading that describes the word. Order of answers for each category may vary.

1. summer
2. winter
3. little
4. October
5. travel*
6. color*
7. apple
8. able
9. November
10. ever
11. later
12. purple

Words That End with /ər/

summer **(1 point)**

winter **(1)**

October **(1)**

color **(1)**

November **(1)**

ever **(1)**

later **(1)**

Words That End with /əl/

little **(1)**

travel **(1)**

apple **(1)**

able **(1)**

purple **(1)**

LOBO

Name _____

Spelling Spree

Crossword Puzzle Write a Spelling Word in the
puzzle that means the same as each clue.

Across

3. the month before
   December **(1)**
4. not big **(1)**
6. the month after
   September **(1)**
7. red or yellow or green **(1)**

Down

1. the hottest season **(1)**
2. take a trip **(1)**
4. the opposite of *sooner* **(1)**
5. a mix of blue and red **(1)**

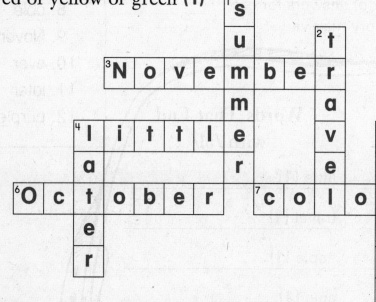

Word Search Write the Spelling Word that
is hidden in each sentence.

   Example: I myse<u>lf lowere</u>d the flag.   **flower**

9. When I take a nap, please be quiet. <u>apple</u> **(1)**

10. The cab lets two people out. <u>able</u> **(1)**

11. Lie very quietly here on the bed. <u>ever</u> **(1)**

12. We'll win terrific prizes! <u>winter</u> **(1)**

Assessment Tip: Total **12** Points

Name _____

Proofreading and Writing

Proofreading Circle the five misspelled Spelling
Words in this paragraph. Then write each word
correctly.

Sarah liked (summir.) It was her favorite time
of year. The heat did not (evir) bother her. Her
parents, however, did not like the heat. They
often wished to (travil) someplace cool. When
Sarah got hot, she rested in the cool kitchen.
Later, she would eat a nice, juicy (appel.) She liked
the fruit's pleasant red (coler) and smooth skin. It
was too bad her parents weren't able to enjoy this
season as much as she did.

Spelling Words

1. summer
2. winter
3. little
4. October
5. travel*
6. color*
7. apple
8. able
9. November
10. ever
11. later
12. purple

1. summer **(2 points)**   4. apple **(2)**

2. ever **(2)**   5. color **(2)**

3. travel **(2)**

Write a Paragraph What can Sarah do to help her parents
stay cool? How can Sarah get her parents to like the summer
as much as she does?

**On a separate sheet of paper, write a paragraph about what
Sarah might do or say to her parents to help them enjoy the
summer. Use Spelling Words from the list.** Responses will vary. **(2)**

Name _____

In Other Words

Choose a synonym for each word from the word box below. Write the synonym in the blanks next to the word. Then write each numbered letter in the matching blanks to solve the puzzle.

Word Bank

foolish	loud	stroll	tugged	yell
frighten	speed	tired	wealth	

1. walk   <u>s</u> <u>t</u> <u>r</u> <u>o</u> <u>l</u> <u>l</u> **(1 point)**
                   1

2. shout   <u>y</u> <u>e</u> <u>l</u> <u>l</u> **(1)**
            3

3. pulled   <u>t</u> <u>u</u> <u>g</u> <u>g</u> <u>e</u> <u>d</u> **(1)**
            6

4. scare   <u>f</u> <u>r</u> <u>i</u> <u>g</u> <u>h</u> <u>t</u> <u>e</u> <u>n</u> **(1)**
                2

5. sleepy   <u>t</u> <u>i</u> <u>r</u> <u>e</u> <u>d</u> **(1)**
             7

6. race   <u>s</u> <u>p</u> <u>e</u> <u>e</u> <u>d</u> **(1)**
      4

7. riches   <u>w</u> <u>e</u> <u>a</u> <u>l</u> <u>t</u> <u>h</u> **(1)**
          5

8. noisy   <u>l</u> <u>o</u> <u>u</u> <u>d</u> **(1)**
        8

9. silly   <u>f</u> <u>o</u> <u>o</u> <u>l</u> <u>i</u> <u>s</u> <u>h</u> **(1)**
               9

This is a word for a book of synonyms:

<u>t</u> <u>h</u> <u>e</u> <u>s</u> <u>a</u> <u>u</u> <u>r</u> <u>u</u> <u>s</u> **(1)**
 1 2 3 4 5 6 7 8 9

Assessment Tip: Total **10** Points

Name _____

Writing with Adjectives

On the lines to the right of each sentence, list the adjectives. Then write each adjective in the chart below.

1. Pepita has one playful dog. ___one; playful **(2 points)**___

2. She has many friendly neighbors. ___many; friendly **(2)**___

3. Pepita has an unusual problem. ___an; unusual **(2)**___

4. She speaks perfect Spanish and English. ___perfect **(2)**___

5. She does not confuse the two languages. ___the; two **(2)**___

6. Pepita gets an angry feeling. ___an; angry **(2)**___

7. Juan teaches Lobo a new trick. ___a; new **(2)**___

8. Mother makes a dozen tacos. ___a; dozen **(2)**___

9. She also prepares some salsa. ___some **(2)**___

10. Pepita learns an important lesson. ___an; important **(2)**___

What Kind?	**How Many?**	**Articles**
playful	one	a
friendly	many	an
unusual	two	the
perfect	dozen	
angry	some	
new		
important		

Name _____

Adjectives in Paragraphs

**Read this paragraph about a neighborhood.
Choose an adjective from the box to complete each
sentence. Use the clues in parentheses to help you.**

Word Bank

an	beautiful	exciting	favorite	full
happy	hundred	long	several	the

Carlos's neighborhood has an _exciting **(1 point)**_

(what kind) block party. Almost a _hundred **(1)**_

(how many) people are there. Many people help to prepare

_an **(1)**_ (article) excellent meal. Two _long **(1)**_

(what kind) tables are covered with _full **(1)**_

(what kind) plates. Carlos and _several **(1)**_

(how many) neighbors sing their _favorite **(1)**_

(what kind) songs. The _beautiful **(1)**_ (what

kind) words are in Spanish. Soon, everyone joins _the **(1)**_

(article) singers. Even the dog woofs a _happy **(1)**_

(what kind) bark at the end of every song.

Assessment Tip: Total **10** Points

Name _____

Expanding Sentences with Adjectives

**Rewrite each sentence. Add at least one adjective to each sentence.
Remember that you may need to change *a* or *an*, too.**

(Answers may vary. Sample answers are included.)

1. Pepita and Juan have a dog.

   Pepita and Juan have a **young** dog. **(1 point)**

2. Pepita goes to a picnic.

   Pepita goes to a **neighborhood** picnic. **(1)**

3. She helps prepare the food.

   She helps prepare the **delicious** food. **(1)**

4. The neighbors sing songs.

   The **friendly** neighbors sing **sweet** songs. **(1)**

5. Lobo almost runs into a truck.

   Lobo almost runs into **an enormous** truck. **(1)**

6. Pepita calls the dog.

   Pepita calls the **naughty** dog. **(1)**

7. The dog hears her shout.

   The **silly** dog hears her **loud** shout. **(1)**

8. She gives Lobo a hug.

   She gives Lobo a **big** hug. **(1)**

Name _____

Announcement Planner

Use this page to organize your ideas for an
announcement. Write an announcement about a birth,
wedding, concert, fair, parade, or other special event.

Who?	What?	Where?	When?	Why?	How?

ANNOUNCEMENT

Responses will vary. **(12 points)**

_____

_____

_____

_____

_____

_____

_____

Assessment Tip: Total **12** Points

Name _____

Ordering Important Information

▶ When writing an announcement, first decide what information is most important. Put that information first.

▶ Put other information in order of importance from most important to least important.

▶ Be sure your announcement includes all the necessary information that answers some or all of these questions: Who? What? Where? When? How? Why?

Number the information in the order it should go in the announcement. Write I for the first thing that should be in the announcement. Write 2 for the second thing. (1 point each)

_2 or 4_ Practice will be at Jamal's house.

_5 or 3_ Practice will end at noon.

_1_____ There will be band practice on Saturday.

_4 or 2_ Practice begins at 10:00 a.m.

_3 or 5_ Jamal's address is 32 Windsor Lane.

Rewrite the announcement in the order you marked.

(3 points)

_____

_____

_____

_____

_____

_____

Name _____

Revising Your Essay

Reread your persuasive essay. What do you need to make it better? Use this page to help you decide. Put a checkmark in the box for each sentence that describes your persuasive essay.

Rings the Bell!

☐ My essay has an attention-grabbing beginning.

☐ I state my goal clearly and give reasons to support it.

☐ I use facts and examples to support my opinion.

☐ The essay is interesting to read and convincing.

Getting Stronger

☐ I could make the beginning more attention grabbing.

☐ I state my goal, but could add reasons to support it.

☐ I need more facts and examples to make it convincing.

☐ There are some run-on sentences I need to fix.

☐ There are a few other mistakes.

Try Harder

☐ I need a better beginning.

☐ I don't state my goals or reasons for my opinion.

☐ I need to add facts and examples.

☐ This isn't very convincing.

☐ There are a lot of mistakes.

Name _____

Correcting Run-On Sentences

**Fix these run-on sentences. Write the sentences correctly
on the lines provided.** Answers will vary. Sample answers given.

1. <u>Run-On</u>: Jane Goodall is one of the world's great scientists,
   she studies chimpanzees.

   <u>Corrected</u>: Jane Goodall is one of the world's great scientists. She studies

   chimpanzees. **(2 points)**

2. <u>Run-On</u>: More than thirty years ago Goodall had an interesting
   idea, she would study chimps in their natural habitat.

   <u>Corrected</u>: More than thirty years ago Goodall had an interesting idea. She

   would study chimps in their natural habitat. **(2)**

3. <u>Run-On</u>: At first, the chimps were suspicious, gradually Goodall
   gained their trust.

   <u>Corrected</u>: At first, the chimps were suspicious. Gradually Goodall gained

   their trust. **(2)**

4. <u>Run-On</u>: Goodall got to know each chimp in the group, each
   chimp was given a name.

   <u>Corrected</u>: Goodall got to know each chimp in the group. Each chimp was

   given a name. **(2)**

5. <u>Run-On</u>: Goodall was the first to discover that chimps made tools,
   she also discovered that chimps could learn new ideas.

   <u>Corrected</u>: Goodall was the first to discover that chimps made tools. She also

   discovered that chimps could learn new ideas. **(2)**

Name _____

Spelling Words

Look for spelling patterns you have learned to help you remember the Spelling Words on this page. Think about the parts that you find hard to spell.

Write the missing letters and apostrophes in the Spelling Words below. Order of answers for 2–3 may vary.

1. h __i__ __s__ **(1 point)**

2. I '__ __d__ **(1)**

3. I '__ __m__ **(1)**

4. th __a__ __t__ '__ __s__ **(1)**

5. did __n__ '__ __t__ **(1)**

6. do __n__ '__ __t__ **(1)**

7. __k__ __n__ ow **(1)**

8. __o__ __u__ tsid __e__ **(1)**

9. b __e__ __e__ n **(1)**

10. we '__ __r__ __e__ **(1)**

11. __a__ nyone **(1)**

12. __a__ nyway **(1)**

Spelling Words

1. his
2. I'd
3. I'm
4. that's
5. didn't
6. don't
7. know
8. outside
9. been
10. we're
11. anyone
12. anyway

Study List On another sheet of paper, write each Spelling Word. Check the list to be sure you spelled each word correctly. Order of words may vary. **(1 point each)**

Assessment Tip: Total **24** Points

Spelling Spree

Contraction Math Add the first word to the second word to get a contraction from the Spelling Word list.

Spelling Words

1. his
2. I'd
3. I'm
4. that's
5. didn't
6. don't
7. know
8. outside
9. been
10. we're
11. anyone
12. anyway

1. do + not = _____
2. we + are = _____
3. that + is = _____
4. I + had = _____
5. did + not = _____
6. I + am = _____

1. don't **(1 point)**
2. we're **(1)**
3. that's **(1)**
4. I'd **(1)**
5. didn't **(1)**
6. I'm **(1)**

Fill in the Blanks Fill each blank in these sentences with the Spelling Word that makes the most sense.

It's freezing __7__! Has __8__ seen my jacket? I've __9__ keeping it on the floor in my room, but it's not there. Now I don't __10__ where it is. Dad said it's not in __11__ study, either. Well __12__, if you see it, let me know.

7. outside **(1)**
8. anyone **(1)**
9. been **(1)**
10. know **(1)**
11. his **(1)**
12. anyway **(1)**

Name _____

Proofreading and Writing

Proofreading Circle the four misspelled Spelling Words in this advertisement. Then write each word correctly.

Do you have a problem that you don't (kno) how to solve? Then call us at Smart Solutions! We've (bin) solving people's problems for over twenty years. And (anywon) will tell you that our prices can't be beat. So give us a call at 555-1971 — (weare) waiting!

1. know **(1 point)**   3. anyone **(1)**

2. been **(1)**   4. we're **(1)**

Write a Caption Draw a picture of a problem that needs to be solved. Then write a caption describing the problem and how to fix it. Use Spelling Words from the list. Responses will vary **(4)**

Assessment Tip: Total **8** Points

Name _____

Sewing Words

Fill in the blanks with the correct word from the Word Bank. (Hint: Not every word will be used.) Then find and circle all the Word Bank words in the puzzle.

Word Bank

fabric	hem	mended	pattern
rustling	plaid	draped	

1. Another word for cloth is <u>fabric **(1 point)**</u> .

2. To make pants shorter, you could <u>hem **(1)**</u> them.

3. A shirt with a hole in it needs to be <u>mended **(1)**</u> .

4. Different-colored stripes that cross one another make a

   design called <u>plaid **(1)**</u> .

5. If you are wearing a shirt with a decorative design on it, the

   shirt has a <u>pattern **(1)**</u> .

(1 point for each word circled in word search.)

```
C R R D R A P E D M Q Y S
F L U B F D A S O G M R E
O T S N A C T T M J P E D
H Q T U B B T Y E G L U C
E M L N R J E M N Y A U A
M C I W I J R P D N I S O
Z U N V C H N S E O D S Z
K E G B Q T W G D W U O I
H E Q E B Y Q J E F P R J
```

Conclusions Chart

Some answers may vary. Examples are given.

Pages	Questions
284–286	1. What is the narrator's name? <u>George **(1 point)**</u> Which story clues helped you? <u>Poppa and the narrator go to the store. The storekeeper</u> <u>says, "Howdy, Poppa. Howdy, George." **(2)**</u>
286	2. How does Poppa feel about plaid pants? <u>He likes them better than plain ones. **(1)**</u> Which story clues helped you? <u>Poppa thinks the plain ones are "poor pickings"; he</u> <u>whistles when he sees the plaid ones. **(2)**</u>
288	3. How does George feel about being kissed by Big Mama and Aunt Viney? <u>He doesn't like it. **(1)**</u> Which story clues helped you? <u>George says that they covered his face with lipstick; he</u> <u>"almost drowned in a sea of sloppy wet kisses." **(2)**</u>
292	4. Who is the first shape? <u>Grandma Tiny **(1)**</u> Which story clues helped you? <u>The first shape is small and white; her name is Tiny. **(2)**</u>

Assessment Tip: Total **12** Points

Name _____

Who, What, and Why?

Use complete sentences to answer the questions about
Poppa's New Pants.

Who comes to visit Grandma Tiny, Poppa, and George?

Aunt Viney and Big Mama come to visit. **(1 point)**

What is wrong with the pants Poppa buys?

They are too long. **(1)**

Why won't the women hem Poppa's pants?

They are too tired. **(1)**

Why does George have trouble getting to sleep?

He is not used to sleeping in the kitchen; the furniture looks scary and makes

scary noises. **(1)**

What weird sights does George see?

He sees three white shapes: one small; one tall, thin, and ghostly; and one big one. **(1)**

What is Grandma Tiny's surprise?

She has hemmed Poppa's pants. **(1)**

Why do the women surprise each other?

They did not know that the others had hemmed the pants too, so now the pants

are too short. **(1)**

Why does George feel lucky about the mix-up?

The pants are the right size for knickers for him. **(1)**

_____

Name _____

Drawing Conclusions

Read the story. Then complete the chart on the next page.

The Pink Sweatshirt

"But Mom, I need a *pink* sweatshirt for our play!" I argued. "I'm the pig who builds with bricks! We need pink sweatshirts with hoods so we can sew on pink felt ears."

"Linda, I just bought you a white sweatshirt," said Mom. "You'll have to spend your own money if you want a pink one."

I was saving all my money for a new bike. "Oh, Mom! Tina's and Ali's parents are buying them pink ones," I whined.

This did not convince my mother. "Lots of pigs aren't pink," she said firmly. "You can be a white pig in a white sweatshirt."

But Tina, Ali, and I wanted our costumes to match. So, I got my new pair of red shorts, the ones labeled, "Wash in COLD WATER only." I dumped those and my white sweatshirt into the washing machine. Then I punched the button marked HOT WATER. Too bad I didn't look in the washer first! The load of white laundry left in there got washed again (in hot water) with my sweatshirt and red shorts.

So, today I'm spending my savings on new white socks for my brother, a white shirt for Dad, and four white towels. Luckily, Dad likes the new color of his bathrobe. It reminds him of a strawberry milkshake.

Name _____

Drawing Conclusions continued

Answer each question about "The Pink Sweatshirt." Then tell which story clues helped you to draw that conclusion.

1. Who is the girl telling the story?

   Linda **(1 point)**

   Story Clues: She is talking to her mom; her mom calls her Linda. **(2)**

   _____

2. What happens when you wash red and white laundry together in hot water?

   Some clothes are dyed pink. **(1)**

   Story Clues: Linda wanted to dye her white sweatshirt pink, so she washed it

   in hot water with her red shorts; the new color of Dad's bathrobe

   reminds him of a strawberry milkshake. **(2)**

3. What other laundry was already in the washing machine?

   There were white socks, a shirt, towels, and a bathrobe. **(1)**

   Story Clues: Linda must buy new socks, shirt, and towels; her dad's bathrobe

   is now pink. **(2)**

4. Why must Linda spend the money she is trying to save?

   Linda must replace the other laundry that turned pink. **(1)**

   Story Clues: A load of laundry was washed again when she washed her

   clothes; Linda has to buy new white socks, shirt, and towels. **(2)**

Name _____

Which One Belongs?

Write the word from the box that belongs in each group.

Word Bank

cover	writer	below	finish	second
siren	female	frozen	shiver	clever

1. instant, moment, <u>second **(1 point)**</u>

2. under, beneath, <u>below **(1)**</u>

3. shake, tremble, <u>shiver **(1)**</u>

4. cold, icy, <u>frozen **(1)**</u>

5. smart, intelligent, <u>clever **(1)**</u>

6. author, poet, <u>writer **(1)**</u>

7. whistle, horn, <u>siren **(1)**</u>

8. hide, cloak, <u>cover **(1)**</u>

9. girl, woman, <u>female **(1)**</u>

10. end, complete, <u>finish **(1)**</u>

Assessment Tip: Total **10** Points

Name _____

Words That Begin
with *a* or *be*

In two-syllable words, the unstressed /ə/ sound at the beginning of a word may be spelled *a*. The unstressed /bĭ/ sounds may be spelled *be*.

/ə/ **a**gain   /bĭ/ **be**fore

Write each Spelling Word under the heading that tells how the word begins. Order of answers for each category may vary.

First Syllable *a*	First Syllable *be*
again **(1 point)**	began **(1)**
around **(1)**	before **(1)**
away **(1)**	because **(1)**
about **(1)**	between **(1)**
alive **(1)**	behind **(1)**
ahead **(1)**	
ago **(1)**	

Name _____

Spelling Spree

Code Breaker Use the code to figure out each
Spelling Word below. Then write the word.

∞ = be   ∧ = a   ⏎ = g
⊗ = n   ∇ = i   _ = o

Example: ∞ t w e e ⊗   between

1. ∧ w ∧ y   away **(1 point)**

2. ∧ b _ u t   about **(1)**

3. ∞ h ∇ ⊗ d   behind **(1)**

4. ∞ c ∧ u s e   because **(1)**

5. ∧ ⏎ ∧ ∇ ⊗   again **(1)**

6. ∧ r _ u ⊗ d   around **(1)**

7. ∞ f _ r e   before **(1)**

Rhyme Time Write a Spelling Word on each line
that rhymes with the name in the sentence.

Example: Where are _____, Faye? they

8. It's _____, Clive. alive **(1)**

9. What's _____, Ned? ahead **(1)**

10. That was long _____, Joe. ago **(1)**

11. We already _____, Jan. began **(1)**

12. Put them in _____, Jean. between **(1)**

Spelling Words

1. began
2. again
3. around
4. before
5. away
6. about
7. alive
8. because
9. ahead
10. between
11. behind
12. ago

Assessment Tip: Total **12** Points

Name _____

Proofreading and Writing

Proofreading Circle the five misspelled Spelling Words in this journal entry. Then write each word correctly.

It all (bigan) after I brought home my fancy new pants. I couldn't wear them (becaus) they were too long. No one (eround) the house could help me make them shorter. Everyone was too tired. Then, (bifor) morning, the pants were too short! Someone got up in the night to fix them. This happened (agin) and then again. Now they are just about perfect for my son.

Spelling Words

1. began
2. again
3. around
4. before
5. away
6. about
7. alive
8. because
9. ahead
10. between
11. behind
12. ago

1. began **(2 points)** _____

2. because **(2)** _____

3. around **(2)** _____

4. before **(2)** _____

5. again **(2)** _____

✏️ **Take a Survey** Ask two or three friends about what others have done to help them. Take notes.

On a separate sheet of paper, write about how people helped your friends. Use Spelling Words from the list. Responses will vary. **(2)**

Theme 6: **Smart Solutions** 149
Assessment Tip: Total **12** Points

Name _____

Antonym Crossword Puzzle

Read each clue. Then choose an antonym from the word bank and fill in the correct boxes on the crossword puzzle. Use a dictionary for help.

Across
2. lost (**1 point**)
4. first (**1**)
6. remember (**1**)
8. thick (**1**)

Down
1. slow (**1**)
3. clean (**1**)
5. short (**1**)
6. plain (**1**)
7. full (**1**)
9. sad (**1**)

Assessment Tip: Total **10** Points

Name _____

Writing Comparisons

Complete this chart with the correct forms of the adjective.

Adjective	Compare Two Things	Compare More Than Two Things
short	shorter	shortest
loud	1. louder **(1 point)**	2. loudest **(1)**
soft	3. softer **(1)**	4. softest **(1)**
bold	5. bolder **(1)**	6. boldest **(1)**
quiet	7. quieter **(1)**	8. quietest **(1)**
sharp	9. sharper **(1)**	10. sharpest **(1)**

Choose a word from the chart to complete each sentence.
Answers may vary. Sample answers are included.

11. The gray fabric is _softer **(1)**_ than the red fabric.

12. Big Mama is the _quietest **(1)**_ ghost.

13. The _loudest **(1)**_ sound came right after midnight.

14. Aunt Viney is a _softer **(1)**_ speaker than
Grandma Tiny.

15. Big Mama takes the _sharpest **(1)**_
needle from her sewing kit.

Theme 6: **Smart Solutions**   151
Assessment Tip: Total **15** Points

Name _____

Writing the Correct Form

**Write the correct form of the adjective in parentheses to
complete each sentence.**

1. Poppa's new pants are <u>longer **(1 point)**</u> than
   his old pants. (long)

2. Big Mama is <u>older **(1)**</u> than her sister. (old)

3. Aunt Viney is the <u>fastest **(1)**</u> sewer of the
   three ghosts. (fast)

4. The snipping sound is <u>louder **(1)**</u> than a
   whisper. (loud)

5. Grandma Tiny is the <u>loudest **(1)**</u> of all. (loud)

6. Poppa is <u>taller **(1)**</u> than George. (tall)

7. George thinks the second ghost is <u>odder **(1)**</u>
   than the first. (odd)

8. Now Poppa's pants are the <u>shortest **(1)**</u>
   pants in the house. (short)

9. George has <u>shorter **(1)**</u> legs
   than Poppa. (short)

10. This story is the <u>weirdest **(1)**</u>
    story I know. (weird)

Assessment Tip: Total **10 Points**

Name _____

A Good Story, Well Told

Using *good* and *well* Suppose George wrote a letter. Proofread the letter. Check that *good* and *well* are used correctly. Check for spelling errors too. Rewrite the letter below.

Dear Cousin,

    Poppa bought a well new pair of pants last week. But they did not fit him good, so Poppa asked Big Mama, Grandma Tiny, and Aunt Viney to hemm the pants. They said no. Poppa was a little sad, but he is a good man. He didn't complain. Guess what happened next! All three women got up in the middle of the night. They each mennded the pants!

    When Poppa woke up, he got a well shock. His new pants had turned into shorts. Luckily, the pants fit me good.

                 Your cousin,
                 George

Dear Cousin,

    Poppa bought a **good (1)** new pair of pants last week. But they did not fit him **well (1)**, so Poppa asked Big Mama, Grandma Tiny, and Aunt Viney to **hem (1)** the pants. They said no. Poppa was a little sad, but he is a good man. He didn't complain. Guess what happened next! All three women got up in the middle of the night. They each **mended (1)** the pants.

    When Poppa woke up, he got a **good (1)** shock. His new pants had turned into shorts. Luckily, the pants fit me **well (1)**.

                 Your cousin,

                 George

Assessment Tip: Total **6** Points

Name _____

Story Map

Use this Story Map to plan a summary of a story you have read recently. Remember to tell who the story is about. Then tell the main things that happened in the story.

Who is the story about?

(2 points)

_____

_____

Problem

(2)

_____

_____

What happens?

(2)

_____

_____

How does it end?

(2)

_____

_____

Name _____

Paraphrasing

► Paraphrasing is restating something in your own words, without changing the author's meaning.

► Writers use paraphrasing when they write a summary or notes for a report.

Circle the letter of the paraphrasing that does not change the author's meaning in the following sentence.

"Grandma Tiny's about to bust a gusset making sure everything's just right."

A. "Grandma Tiny is working hard to make sure everything is just right."

B. "Grandma Tiny is working so hard that she broke something."

Paraphrase each sentence: Answers may vary.

1. Aunt Viney and Big Mama took turns covering my face with red lipstick.

   Aunt Viney and Big Mama took turns kissing me. **(2 points)**

2. Grandma Tiny, Big Mama, and Aunt Viney usually have a good long gossip spell when they get together.

   Grandma Tiny, Big Mama, and Aunt Viney usually gossip a lot

   when they get together. **(2)**

3. I stayed balled up under those blankets like an armadillo for the rest of the night.

   I stayed curled up under the blankets for the rest of the night. **(2)**

4. Grandma Tiny was smiling fit to beat the band.

   Grandma Tiny was beaming. **(2)**

Name _____

A Rainy-Day Survey!

Write sentences to answer the following questions.

Answers will vary. Sample answers are provided.

1. Do you think rainy days are **dismal** and **dreary**? Why or why not?

   Yes, because I like to play outside, but not when it rains. **(2 points)**

   _____

2. On days when the rain is **ceaseless**, what do you do?

   I stay inside and read. **(2)**

   _____

3. Do you like the sound of rain **pelting** against your window?

   Yes, because it helps me fall asleep. **(2)**

   _____

4. What do you do when you feel **companionable**?

   I play with my friends. **(2)**

   _____

5. What advice would you give to a friend who feels **discouraged**?

   I would tell her to cheer up! **(2)**

   _____

6. What activity makes you feel **exhausted**?

   I feel exhausted after I play a game of soccer. **(2)**

   _____

Name _____

Generalizations Chart

Answers will vary. Examples are given.

Rainy Days	**Older Sisters**
unending rain pelting down **(1 point)** family members are cross and grouchy **(1)** cleaning her room is a boring chore for Ramona **(1)**	Beezus mysteriously moody **(1)** doesn't have to clean her room when Ramona does **(1)** stalks around the house not speaking to anyone **(1)**
Parents	**Restaurants**
mother and father nag Ramona to clean her room **(1)** mother's tone of voice hurts Ramona's feelings **(1)** father jokes about price of fuel oil **(1)** father decides to treat family to dinner at Whopperburger **(1)**	wait to be seated **(1)** order from menu **(1)** served by waitress **(1)** leave tip **(1)**

In general, what statement can you make about people's feelings on rainy days?

Example: A rainy day often makes people feel grumpy. **(1)**

_____

Name _____

Ramona's Diary

Suppose Ramona kept a diary. Finish this entry with details from
Ramona Quimby, Age 8.   Answers may vary. Examples are given.

Dear Diary,

Sunday afternoon was <u>dismal and rainy **(1 point)**</u>.

Mom and Dad were <u>sorting bills and studying; tired, cross, grouchy **(1)**</u>.

Mom kept reminding me to <u>clean my room **(1)**</u>.

Then Beezus asked Mom to <u>let her sleep over at Mary Jane's house **(1)**</u>

<u>   </u>. But Mom and Dad

said no, so Beezus was upset.

Then Dad decided that we should go to the Whopperburger.

He wanted us to <u>stop grumping around; have a treat **(1)**</u>.

While we were waiting for our seats, <u>I didn't like being teased by an</u>

<u>old man **(1)**</u>. Dinner was really tasty

and fun too!

Before the man left, he <u>paid for our dinners without telling us **(1)**</u>

<u>   </u>. On the way home, all

of us were <u>happier; in better moods **(1)**</u>.

Assessment Tip: Total **8** Points

Name _____

Making Cafeteria Food

Read the story below. Then answer the questions on the next page.

Ms. Mallard and Meatloaf

Luis dropped his lunch tray on the table next to his friend Joey and sat down. "Can you believe this? They call this meatloaf!" Luis said. "And they just served it two weeks ago! I can't stand it."

"Then why don't you ask someone why it's always on the menu, Luis?" Joey replied. "All you do is complain."

"You're right. I will." Luis stood up and walked directly back to the serving line where the lunch lady was cleaning up. "Um, Ms. Mallard? Can I ask you something?"

Ms. Mallard turned around. "Ah, yes, of course, Luis. What is it? Enjoying your meatloaf?"

"Not really. That's why I'm here. How come you serve it every two weeks and why does it taste so strange?"

"Well, Luis, schools have rules about the kinds of food we serve," Ms. Mallard responded. "We need to make food that fits in the basic food groups. Meatloaf fits most of them, it's easy to make a lot of, and it doesn't cost much to make. That's why many schools put it on their menus."

"Okay, I get it. But how come it tastes so funny?"

"I can tell you, Luis, that you're not alone on this one. Last summer I went to a national meeting about cafeteria food. Almost everybody I talked to said how much the kids dislike the taste of meatloaf. It probably has something to do with the onions and the peppers in it. Not to mention the dry bread that goes in it. Some people just look at its color and think it can't taste good. That's why. Just try putting ketchup on it."

Name _____

Making Cafeteria Food continued

Answer the following questions based on the story "Ms. Mallard and Meatloaf." Answers will vary.
Examples are given.

What broad statement can you make about schools and meatloaf?

Many schools serve meatloaf. **(2 points)**

What details support your generalization?

Schools have to serve food that fits into the food groups.

Meatloaf fits many of the food groups.

It's easy to make a lot of it.

It's cheap to make. **(4)**

In general, what can you say about kids and the school meatloaf?

Many kids don't like eating the school meatloaf. **(2)**

What details support your generalization?

Everybody from all over the country said that kids don't like its taste.

Meatloaf has onions and peppers in it.

It has dry bread in it.

The color of it makes some people think it doesn't taste good. **(4)**

---

160   Theme 6: **Smart Solutions**
Assessment Tip: Total **12** Points

Name _____

Contraction Puzzler

What did Ramona learn on that rainy Sunday? Solve the puzzle to find out. Write the two words that each contraction is made from. Write only one letter on each line. Then write each numbered letter on the line with the matching number below.

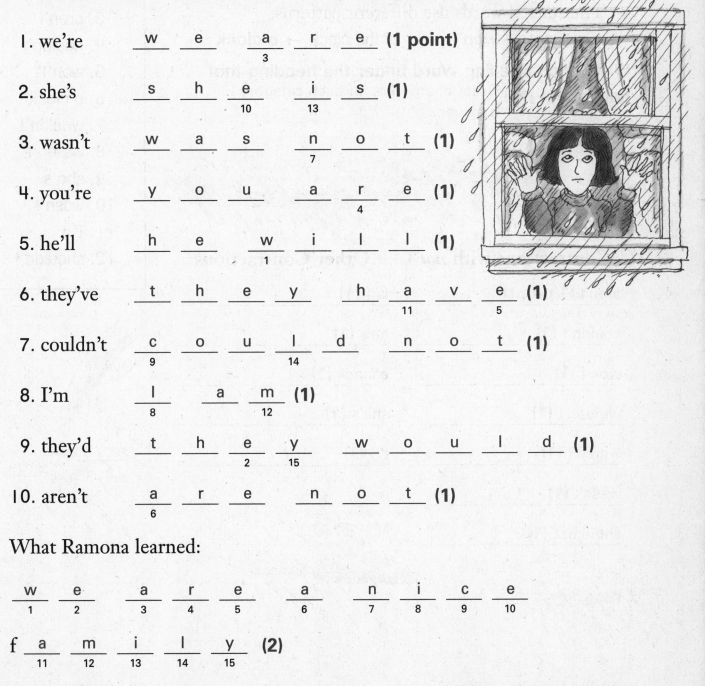

1. we're   w   e   a   r   e   **(1 point)**
                      3

2. she's   s   h   e   i   s   **(1)**
                      10   13

3. wasn't   w   a   s   n   o   t   **(1)**
                          7

4. you're   y   o   u   a   r   e   **(1)**
                              4

5. he'll   h   e   w   i   l   l   **(1)**
                      1

6. they've   t   h   e   y   h   a   v   e   **(1)**
                              11   5

7. couldn't   c   o   u   l   d   n   o   t   **(1)**
              9   14

8. I'm   I   a   m   **(1)**
              8   12

9. they'd   t   h   e   y   w   o   u   l   d   **(1)**
                  2   15

10. aren't   a   r   e   n   o   t   **(1)**
              6

What Ramona learned:

w   e   a   r   e   a   n   i   c   e
1   2   3   4   5   6   7   8   9   10

f   a   m   i   l   y   **(2)**
    11 12 13 14 15

Name _____

Contractions

A contraction is a short way of saying or writing two or more words. An apostrophe takes the place of one or more letters.

I am → **I'm**   are not → **aren't**

► The starred words use different patterns.

will not → **won't**   of the clock → **o'clock**

Write each Spelling Word under the heading that tells about it. Order of answers for each category may vary.

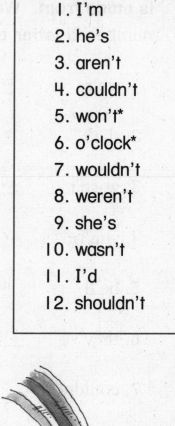

Spelling Words

1. I'm
2. he's
3. aren't
4. couldn't
5. won't*
6. o'clock*
7. wouldn't
8. weren't
9. she's
10. wasn't
11. I'd
12. shouldn't

Contractions with *not*

aren't **(1 point)**

couldn't **(1)**

won't **(1)**

wouldn't **(1)**

weren't **(1)**

wasn't **(1)**

shouldn't **(1)**

Other Contractions

I'm **(1)**

he's **(1)**

o'clock **(1)**

she's **(1)**

I'd **(1)**

Assessment Tip: Total **12** Points

Name _____

Spelling Spree

Book Titles Write the Spelling Word that best completes each funny book title. Remember to use capital letters.

Spelling Words

1. I'm
2. he's
3. aren't
4. couldn't
5. won't
6. o'clock*
7. wouldn't
8. weren't
9. she's
10. wasn't
11. I'd
12. shouldn't

> **Example:** *No Puzzle I _____ or Wouldn't Solve* by
> I. M. Smarte Couldn't

1. *The Clock Stopped at One _____* by Minnie T. Hand
2. *_____ You Glad I'm Here?* by Happy A. Ginn
3. *_____ My Brother: A True Story* by N. O. Kidding
4. *The Man Who _____ a Spy* by Minny Kluze

1. O'Clock **(1 point)**

2. Aren't **(1)**

3. He's **(1)**

4. Wasn't **(1)**

Make It Shorter Circle the words below that could be written as contractions. Then write them as contractions on the lines.

5. Mom (would not) let you do that.

6. You (should not) even ask her.

7. (She is) reading the paper.

8. It (was not) a good idea.

5. wouldn't **(1)**

6. shouldn't **(1)**

7. She's **(1)**

8. wasn't **(1)**

Name _____

Proofreading and Writing

Proofreading Suppose Ramona wrote a note.
Circle the five misspelled Spelling Words in the note.
Then write each word correctly.

1. I'm
2. he's
3. aren't
4. couldn't
5. won't*
6. o'clock*
7. wouldn't
8. weren't
9. she's
10. wasn't
11. I'd
12. shouldn't

Sunday, 8 o'clock
Dear Mom and Dad,

(Id) like to thank you for taking us to the Whopperburger. We (were'nt) having a good day until then. Even Beezus is happier now, but she (woen't) admit it. Aren't you glad the old man was there? I (could'nt) believe that he paid for our meal. (I'am) glad we're a family.
Love,
Ramona

1. I'd **(2 points)**

2. weren't **(2)**

3. won't **(2)**

4. couldn't **(2)**

5. I'm **(2)**

✏️ **Write a Skit** Choose a scene to act out from *Ramona Quimby, Age 8,* or make up your own scene with two people from her family.

Write the words that the characters might say to each other. Use Spelling Words from the list. Responses will vary. **(2)**

Assessment Tip: Total **12** Points

Name _____

Find the Correct Word

Write the missing word in each sentence. A sample word at the end of each sentence gives a clue about the vowel sound. Find the correct word on the word list and write it in the blank. Then circle the letters in the word that match the vowel sound in the sample word. Look at the spelling table for help.

Word Bank

scent

south

dough

foil

hood

heat

1. The furnace will heat **(1 point)** _____ the

   whole house. **beast**

2. Lin put on her gloves and hood **(1)** _____

   in the snowstorm. **good**

3. The foil **(1)** _____ kept my sandwich fresh. **join**

4. The cook placed the pie dough **(1)** _____
   into a pan. **though**

5. Birds fly south **(1)** _____ when the weather
   gets cold. **house**

6. What is that lovely scent **(1)** _____ coming
   from the kitchen? **went**

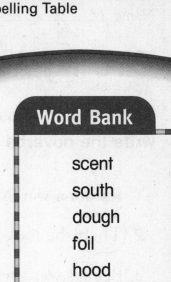

Spelling Table

/ă/ bat	/ē/ beast	/ŏ/ pond	/o͝o/ good
/ā/ play	/ĭ/ give	/ō/ though	/o͞o/ house
/â/ care	/ī/ time	/ô/ paw	
/ĕ/ went	/î/ near	/oi/ join	

Name _____

Circling Adverbially

Circle the adverbs in each sentence. Then write the adverbs in the chart below.

1. Ramona watches the rain (sadly.) **(1 point)**

2. (Then) she looks (around) in the kitchen. **(2)**

3. Beezus was crying (loudly) (upstairs.) **(2)**

4. (Next,) Mrs. Quimby (gently) scolded Ramona. **(2)**

5. (Nearby,) Mr. Quimby read his book (silently.) **(2)**

6. Ramona (often) reads stories to Willa Jean. **(1)**

7. The pelting rain falls (everywhere.) **(1)**

8. "I wanted to bicycle (today,") she thought (sulkily.) **(2)**

9. (Finally,) Mr. Quimby decided to cheer everyone up. **(1)**

10. They decided to eat (out) at Whopperburger. **(1)**

How	When	Where
sadly	then	around
loudly	next	upstairs
gently	often	nearby
silently	today	everywhere
sulkily	finally	out

Assessment Tip: Total **15** Points

Choosing Adverbs

Choose an adverb from the box to complete each sentence. Use the clue in parentheses to help you.

around
completely
inside
loudly
often
out
quickly
sharply
slowly
quietly

Mr. Quimby parked the car and the family walked

inside **(1)** _____ (where). The customers

filled the restaurant completely **(1)** _____ (how).

Ramona and Beezus quarreled loudly **(1)** _____

(how). Mrs. Quimby scolded them sharply **(1)** _____

(how). When they were seated, they ordered

quickly **(1)** _____ (how). Soon the waitress

appeared. She carried platters of food

out **(1)** _____ (where) of the kitchen.

The Quimbys sat at the table

quietly **(1)** _____ (how). Ramona ate

slowly **(1)** _____ (how). She wished the

meal could last forever. She often **(1)** _____

(when) wished for impossible things. Ramona

looked around **(1)** _____ (where).
She wanted to remember her perfect meal.

Name _____

Expanding Sentences with Adverbs

Add one adverb to each sentence. In the first five sentences, add the adverb in the blank. Use the clues in parentheses to help you. In the other sentences, decide where to add the adverb.
Answers may vary. Sample answers are supplied.

1. Mother talks <u>strictly **(1 point)**</u> to Becky. (how)

2. Mother <u>often **(1)**</u> talks to Becky. (when)

3. Becky looks <u>everywhere **(1)**</u> for Fluffy. (where)

4. "I want to sleep over at Mimi's," Susan shouted
   <u>angrily **(1)**</u>. (how)

5. <u>Soon **(1)**</u> Susan was in tears. (when)

6. Susan slammed her door.

   <u>Susan slammed her door loudly. **(1)**</u>

7. Becky had listened to the quarrel.

   <u>Becky had secretly listened to the quarrel. **(1)**</u>

8. She decided to talk to Susan.

   <u>Then she decided to talk to Susan. **(1)**</u>

9. "May I come in?" asked Becky.

   <u>"May I come in?" asked Becky quietly. **(1)**</u>

10. "Sure," said Susan, "I will only talk to you and our cat."

    <u>"Sure," said Susan quickly, "I will only talk to you and our cat." **(1)**</u>

Name _____

Planning Your Personal Essay

Use this graphic organizer to help you plan your personal essay. Write your main idea in the top box. Then write two reasons or facts about your idea in the boxes below. Think of details and examples for each reason. Then summarize your main idea in the last box.

My Main Idea:

(2 points)

_____

_____

Reason 1:

(2)

_____

_____

Reason 2:

(2)

_____

_____

Reason 1 Examples and Details:

(2)

_____

_____

_____

Reason 2 Examples and Details:

(2)

_____

_____

_____

Summary and restatement of main idea:

(2)

_____

_____

Name _____

Telling More with Adverbs

Adverbs can modify verbs. Good writers use adverbs to
tell more about an action. They can tell *how* or *when*.

> The cat is meowing.
> The cat is meowing **loudly**. (tells *how*)
> The cat is meowing **now**. (tells *when*)

Adverbs That Tell How		Adverbs That Tell When	
sadly	patiently	always	tomorrow
silently	secretly	finally	now
loudly	quickly	never	daily
slowly		yesterday	

Rewrite each sentence by adding an adverb to tell how or when.
Sample answers shown.

1. The family ate their meals together (when) <u>daily **(1 point)**</u>.

2. Ginger stared (how) <u>silently **(1)**</u> out
   the window.

3. The log in the fireplace snapped (how) <u>loudly **(1)**</u>.

4. The family waited (how) <u>patiently **(1)**</u>
   for a table in the restaurant.

5. The man went to the store (when) <u>yesterday **(1)**</u>.

6. The girl (how) <u>secretly **(1)**</u> wished for a
   for a bicycle.

7. He (when) <u>never **(1)**</u> told them about it.

8. The dog ran (how) <u>quickly **(1)**</u> past the house.

Assessment Tip: Total **8** Points

Name _____

Writing a Story

Use what you have learned about taking tests to help you write a story. Take some time to plan what you will write. This practice will help you when you take this kind of test.

In *Pepita Talks Twice*, Pepita decides how to solve her problem. Then she realizes her decision is a bad one. She will miss out on many important things if she sticks to her decision. Write a story about someone who needs to find a smart solution to a problem.

Answers will vary. **(15 points)**

_____

_____

_____

_____

_____

_____

_____

_____

_____

_____

_____

Name _____

Writing a Story continued

Read your story. Check to be sure that

- the beginning introduces the characters, the setting, and the problem
- details bring the story to life
- the events are in an order that makes sense
- the ending tells how the problem works out
- there are few mistakes in capitalization, punctuation, grammar, or spelling

Now pick one way to improve your story. Make your changes below.

Answers will vary. **(5)**

_____

_____

_____

_____

_____

_____

_____

_____

_____

_____

_____

_____

Assessment Tip: Total 20 Points

Spelling Review

**Write Spelling Words from the list on this page to
answer the questions.** Order of answers in each
category may vary.

Spelling Words

1–8. Which eight words end with *er* or *le*?

1. ever **(1 point)**

2. little **(1)**

3. purple **(1)**

4. November **(1)**

5. later **(1)**

6. apple **(1)**

7. summer **(1)**

8. able **(1)**

9–14. Which six words begin like the word *asleep*?

9. ago **(1)**

10. around **(1)**

11. again **(1)**

12. about **(1)**

13. away **(1)**

14. alive **(1)**

15–17. Which three words begin with *be*?

15. because **(1)**

16. before **(1)**

17. behind **(1)**

18–25. Which eight words are contractions?

18. I'm **(1)**

19. wasn't **(1)**

20. I'd **(1)**

21. shouldn't **(1)**

22. aren't **(1)**

23. wouldn't **(1)**

24. couldn't **(1)**

25. he's **(1)**

Spelling Words

1. I'm
2. ago
3. ever
4. around
5. wasn't
6. because
7. little
8. I'd
9. purple
10. again
11. shouldn't
12. November
13. about
14. aren't
15. later
16. apple
17. wouldn't
18. away
19. alive
20. summer
21. before
22. couldn't
23. behind
24. he's
25. able

Name _____

Spelling Spree

Complete the Sentence **Fill in the blanks with Spelling Words.**

1. My favorite color is <u>purple **(1 point)**</u>.

2. Thanksgiving is in <u>November **(1)**</u>.

3. Let's have some <u>apple **(1)**</u> pie.

4. The mouse ran <u>away **(1)**</u> from the cat.

5. Margo hid <u>behind **(1)**</u> a bush.

6. I put on my socks <u>before **(1)**</u> my shoes.

Contraction Action **Replace the underlined words with a Spelling Word that is a contraction.**

7. <u>I am</u> <u>I'm **(1)**</u> going to the game with Rico.

8. This is the team <u>I would</u> <u>I'd **(1)**</u> like to be on.

9. <u>He is</u> <u>He's **(1)**</u> the best player on the team.

10. Our uniforms <u>are not</u> <u>aren't **(1)**</u> very clean now.

11. Last year I <u>could not</u> <u>couldn't **(1)**</u> run as fast as Kara.

12. We all know we <u>should not</u> <u>shouldn't **(1)**</u> eat before we swim.

13. Coach <u>would not</u> <u>wouldn't **(1)**</u> let us skip practice.

14. The new game <u>was not</u> <u>wasn't **(1)**</u> hard.

Spelling Words

1. away
2. shouldn't
3. he's
4. before
5. November
6. wouldn't
7. apple
8. wasn't
9. aren't
10. purple
11. couldn't
12. behind
13. I'd
14. I'm

Assessment Tip: Total **14** Points

Name _____

Proofreading and Writing

Proofreading Circle the five misspelled Spelling Words in this message. Write each word correctly.

Playing soccer is better than hanging (arownd.)

Being on a team is great (becuase) you make new

friends. Two years (aggo) I was on a team. Now I

want to play (agin.) It is (abowt) time for tryouts.

Spelling Words

1. around
2. ago
3. again
4. about
5. because
6. summer
7. before
8. ever
9. later
10. little
11. able
12. alive

1. around **(1 point)**   4. again **(1)**

2. because **(1)**   5. about **(1)**

3. ago **(1)**

The Team News Write the Spelling Word that means nearly the opposite of each underlined word or words.

Our team practiced hard this 6. winter summer **(1)** .

We wanted to be ready 7. after before **(1)** the first game.

We knew if we 8. never ever **(1)** wanted to win, we

would have to work. We ended practice 9. earlier later **(1)**

every day. We didn't just practice a 10. lot little **(1)** . We

have put last year's season 11. in front of behind **(1)** us.

Now we hope to be 12. unable able **(1)** to win.

Write an Invitation On a separate sheet of paper, write an invitation to a friend to join a team or club. Use the Spelling Review Words. **(3)**

Responses will vary.

Student Handbook

Contents

How to Study a Word

1. LOOK at the word.
 ► What does the word mean?
 ► What letters are in the word?
 ► Name and touch each letter.

2. SAY the word.
 ► Listen for the consonant sounds.
 ► Listen for the vowel sounds.

3. THINK about the word.
 ► How is each sound spelled?
 ► Close your eyes and picture the word.
 ► What familiar spelling patterns do you see?
 ► What other words have the same spelling patterns?

4. WRITE the word.
 ► Think about the sounds and the letters.
 ► Form the letters correctly.

5. CHECK the spelling.
 ► Did you spell the word the same way it is spelled in your word list?
 ► If you did not spell the word correctly, write the word again.

about	don't	I'd		
again	down	I'll		
almost		I'm	outside	tonight
a lot	enough	into		too
also	every	its	people	two
always	everybody	it's	pretty	
am				until
and	family	January	really	
another	favorite		right	very
anyone	February	knew		
anyway	field	know	said	want
around	finally		Saturday	was
	for	letter	school	Wednesday
beautiful	found	like	some	we're
because	friend	little	something	where
been	from	lose	started	while
before		lying	stopped	who
brought	getting		sure	whole
buy	girl	might	swimming	world
	goes	morning		would
cannot	going	mother	than	wouldn't
can't	guess	myself	that's	write
clothes			their	writing
coming	happily	never	them	
could	have	new	then	you
cousin	haven't	now	there	your
	heard		they	
does	her	off	thought	
didn't	here	one	through	
different	his	other	to	
done	how	our	today	

Seal Surfer

Adding Endings

care − e + ed = car**ed**

save − e + ing = sav**ing**

wrap + p + ed = wrap**ped**

grin + n + ing = grin**ning**

baby − y + ies = bab**ies**

carry − y + ied = carr**ied**

Spelling Words

1. cared
2. babies
3. chopped
4. saving
5. carried
6. fixing
7. hurried
8. joking
9. grinning
10. smiled
11. wrapped
12. parties

Challenge Words

1. moving
2. libraries

My Study List
Add your own spelling words on the back.➡

Animal Habitats
Reading-Writing Workshop

Look for familiar spelling patterns in these words to help you remember their spellings.

Spelling Words

1. girl
2. they
3. want
4. was
5. into
6. who
7. our
8. new
9. would
10. could
11. a lot
12. buy

Challenge Words

1. wouldn't
2. world
3. through
4. while

My Study List
Add your own spelling words on the back.➡

Nights of the Pufflings

The Vowel + /r/ Sounds in *hair*

/âr/ ➡ c**are**, h**air**, b**ear**

Spelling Words

1. hair
2. care
3. chair
4. pair
5. bear
6. where
7. scare
8. air
9. pear
10. bare
11. fair
12. share

Challenge Words

1. flair
2. farewell

My Study List
Add your own spelling words on the back.➡

Name _____

My Study List

1. _____
2. _____
3. _____
4. _____
5. _____
6. _____
7. _____
8. _____
9. _____
10. _____

Review Words

1. buy
2. could

How to Study a Word

Look at the word.
Say the word.
Think about the word.
Write the word.
Check the spelling.

182

Name _____

My Study List

1. _____
2. _____
3. _____
4. _____
5. _____
6. _____
7. _____
8. _____
9. _____
10. _____

How to Study a Word

Look at the word.
Say the word.
Think about the word.
Write the word.
Check the spelling.

182

Name _____

My Study List

1. _____
2. _____
3. _____
4. _____
5. _____
6. _____
7. _____
8. _____
9. _____
10. _____

Review Words

1. making
2. stopped

How to Study a Word

Look at the word.
Say the word.
Think about the word.
Write the word.
Check the spelling.

182

Across the Wide Dark Sea

The Vowel Sounds in *tooth* **and** *cook*

/ōo/ → t**oo**th, ch**ew**

/ŏo/ → c**oo**k

Spelling Words

1. tooth
2. chew
3. grew
4. cook
5. shoe
6. blue
7. boot
8. flew
9. shook
10. balloon
11. drew
12. spoon

Challenge Words

1. loose
2. brook

My Study List
Add your own spelling words on the back. ➡

Animal Habitats Spelling Review

Spelling Words

1. pair
2. unhurt
3. grinning
4. air
5. smiled
6. sadly
7. care
8. retell
9. babies
10. bear
11. unlike
12. cared
13. scare
14. hopeful
15. parties
16. pear
17. remake
18. chopped
19. bare
20. unhappy
21. joking
22. chair
23. friendly
24. carried
25. helper

See the back for Challenge Words

My Study List
Add your own spelling words on the back. ➡

Two Days in May

Prefixes and Suffixes

re + make = **re**make

un + happy = **un**happy

care + **ful** = care**ful**

friend + **ly** = friend**ly**

help + **er** = help**er**

Spelling Words

1. helper
2. unfair
3. friendly
4. unhappy
5. remake
6. careful
7. hopeful
8. unlike
9. retell
10. sadly
11. farmer
12. unhurt

Challenge Words

1. unimportant
2. silently

My Study List
Add your own spelling words on the back. ➡

Take-Home Word List

Name ______________

My Study List

1. ______________
2. ______________
3. ______________
4. ______________
5. ______________
6. ______________
7. ______________
8. ______________
9. ______________
10. ______________

Review Words

1. have
2. said

How to Study a Word

Look at the word.
Say the word.
Think about the word.
Write the word.
Check the spelling.

Take-Home Word List

Name ______________

My Study List

1. ______________
2. ______________
3. ______________
4. ______________
5. ______________
6. ______________
7. ______________
8. ______________
9. ______________
10. ______________

Challenge Words

1. farewell
2. flair
3. moving
4. libraries
5. silently

How to Study a Word

Look at the word.
Say the word.
Think about the word.
Write the word.
Check the spelling.

Take-Home Word List

Name ______________

My Study List

1. ______________
2. ______________
3. ______________
4. ______________
5. ______________
6. ______________
7. ______________
8. ______________
9. ______________
10. ______________

Review Words

1. good
2. soon

How to Study a Word

Look at the word.
Say the word.
Think about the word.
Write the word.
Check the spelling.

Trapped by the Ice!

The VCCV Pattern

VC | CV

Mon | day

sud | den

Spelling Words

1. Monday
2. sudden
3. until
4. forget
5. happen
6. follow
7. dollar
8. window
9. hello
10. market
11. pretty
12. order

Challenge Words

1. stubborn
2. expect

My Study List
Add your own spelling words on the back. →

Yunmi and Halmoni's Trip

The Vowel Sound in *bought*

/ô/ → b**ough**t,

c**augh**t

Spelling Words

1. caught
2. thought
3. bought
4. laugh
5. through
6. enough
7. fought
8. daughter
9. taught
10. brought
11. ought
12. cough

Challenge Words

1. sought
2. granddaughter

My Study List
Add your own spelling words on the back. →

Voyagers Reading-Writing Workshop

Look for familiar spelling patterns in these words to help you remember their spellings.

Spelling Words

1. down
2. how
3. its
4. coming
5. stopped
6. started
7. wrote
8. swimming
9. from
10. write
11. writing
12. brought

Challenge Words

1. favorite
2. sure
3. clothes
4. heard

My Study List
Add your own spelling words on the back. →

Take-Home Word List

Take-Home Word List

Take-Home Word List

Name _____

Name _____

Name _____

My Study List

1. _____
2. _____
3. _____
4. _____
5. _____
6. _____
7. _____
8. _____
9. _____
10. _____

My Study List

1. _____
2. _____
3. _____
4. _____
5. _____
6. _____
7. _____
8. _____
9. _____
10. _____

Review Words

1. teeth
2. was

My Study List

1. _____
2. _____
3. _____
4. _____
5. _____
6. _____
7. _____
8. _____
9. _____
10. _____

Review Words

1. after
2. funny

How to Study a Word

Look at the word.
Say the word.
Think about the word.
Write the word.
Check the spelling.

How to Study a Word

Look at the word.
Say the word.
Think about the word.
Write the word.
Check the spelling.

How to Study a Word

Look at the word.
Say the word.
Think about the word.
Write the word.
Check the spelling.

Smart Solutions
Reading-Writing Workshop

Look for familiar spelling patterns in these words to help you remember their spellings.

Spelling Words

1. his
2. I'd
3. I'm
4. that's
5. didn't
6. don't
7. know
8. outside
9. been
10. we're
11. anyone
12. anyway

Challenge Words

1. lose
2. finally
3. different
4. happily

My Study List
Add your own spelling words on the back. ➡

Pepita Talks Twice

Words That End with *er* or *le*
/ər/ ➡ summ**er**
/əl/ ➡ litt**le**

Spelling Words

1. summer
2. winter
3. little
4. October
5. travel
6. color
7. apple
8. able
9. November
10. ever
11. later
12. purple

Challenge Words

1. thermometer
2. mumble

My Study List
Add your own spelling words on the back. ➡

Voyagers
Spelling Review

Spelling Words

1. grew
2. daughter
3. until
4. cook
5. ought
6. forget
7. balloon
8. caught
9. dollar
10. boot
11. window
12. taught
13. flew
14. brought
15. hello
16. tooth
17. Monday
18. pretty
19. chew
20. sudden
21. order
22. spoon
23. thought
24. happen
25. bought

See the back for Challenge Words

My Study List
Add your own spelling words on the back. ➡

Name _____

My Study List

1. _____
2. _____
3. _____
4. _____
5. _____
6. _____
7. _____
8. _____
9. _____
10. _____

Challenge Words

1. brook
2. expect
3. loose
4. stubborn
5. granddaughter

How to Study a Word

Look at the word.
Say the word.
Think about the word.
Write the word.
Check the spelling.

188

Name _____

My Study List

1. _____
2. _____
3. _____
4. _____
5. _____
6. _____
7. _____
8. _____
9. _____
10. _____

Review Words

1. flower
2. people

How to Study a Word

Look at the word.
Say the word.
Think about the word.
Write the word.
Check the spelling.

188

Name _____

My Study List

1. _____
2. _____
3. _____
4. _____
5. _____
6. _____
7. _____
8. _____
9. _____
10. _____

How to Study a Word

Look at the word.
Say the word.
Think about the word.
Write the word.
Check the spelling.

188

Smart Solutions
Spelling Review

Spelling Words

1. little
2. again
3. summer
4. alive
5. purple
6. around
7. I'm
8. able
9. wouldn't
10. ago
11. ever
12. before
13. aren't
14. I'd
15. because
16. wouldn't
17. away
18. couldn't
19. November
20. shouldn't
21. apple
22. about
23. behind
24. wasn't
25. later

See the back for Challenge Words

My Study List
Add your own spelling words on the back. ➡

Ramona Quimby, Age 8

Contractions
A **contraction** is a short way of writing two or more words. An apostrophe replaces any dropped letters.

Spelling Words

1. I'm
2. he's
3. aren't
4. couldn't
5. won't
6. o'clock
7. wouldn't
8. weren't
9. she's
10. wasn't
11. I'd
12. shouldn't

Challenge Words

1. let's
2. who's

My Study List
Add your own spelling words on the back. ➡

Poppa's New Pants

Words That Begin with *a* or *be*

/ə/ ➡ **a**gain
/bĭ/ ➡ **be**fore

Spelling Words

1. began
2. again
3. around
4. before
5. away
6. about
7. alive
8. because
9. ahead
10. between
11. behind
12. ago

Challenge Words

1. awhile
2. beyond

My Study List
Add your own spelling words on the back. ➡

Name _____

My Study List

1. _____
2. _____
3. _____
4. _____
5. _____
6. _____
7. _____
8. _____
9. _____
10. _____

Review Words

1. they
2. want

How to Study a Word

Look at the word.
Say the word.
Think about the word.
Write the word.
Check the spelling.

Name _____

My Study List

1. _____
2. _____
3. _____
4. _____
5. _____
6. _____
7. _____
8. _____
9. _____
10. _____

Review Words

1. can't
2. isn't

How to Study a Word

Look at the word.
Say the word.
Think about the word.
Write the word.
Check the spelling.

Name _____

My Study List

1. _____
2. _____
3. _____
4. _____
5. _____
6. _____
7. _____
8. _____
9. _____
10. _____

Challenge Words

1. mumble
2. let's
3. awhile
4. who's
5. thermometer

How to Study a Word

Look at the word.
Say the word.
Think about the word.
Write the word.
Check the spelling.

Problem Words

Words	Rules	Examples
are our	*Are* is a verb. *Our* is a possessive pronoun.	<u>Are</u> these gloves yours? This is <u>our</u> car.
doesn't don't	Use *doesn't* with singular nouns, *he*, *she*, and *it*. Use *don't* with plural nouns, *I*, *you*, *we*, and *they*.	Dad <u>doesn't</u> swim. We <u>don't</u> swim.
good well	Use the adjective *good* to describe nouns. Use the adverb *well* to describe verbs.	The weather looks <u>good</u>. She sings <u>well</u>.
its it's	*Its* is a possessive pronoun. *It's* means "*it is*" (contraction).	The dog wagged <u>its</u> tail. <u>It's</u> cold today.
let leave	*Let* means "to allow." *Leave* means "to go away from" or "to let stay."	Please <u>let</u> me go swimming. I will <u>leave</u> soon. <u>Leave</u> it on my desk.
set sit	*Set* means "to put." *Sit* means "to rest or stay in one place."	<u>Set</u> the vase on the table. Please <u>sit</u> in this chair.
their there they're	*Their* means "belonging to them." *There* means "at or in that place." *They're* means "*they are*" (contraction).	<u>Their</u> coats are on the bed. Is Carlos <u>there</u>? <u>They're</u> going to the store.
two to too	*Two* is a number. *To* means "toward." *Too* means "also" or "more than enough."	I bought <u>two</u> shirts. A cat ran <u>to</u> the tree. Can we go <u>too</u>? I ate <u>too</u> many peas.
your you're	*Your* is a possessive pronoun. *You're* means "*you are*" (contraction).	Are these <u>your</u> glasses? <u>You're</u> late again!

Read each question below. Then check your paper. Correct any mistakes you find. After you have corrected them, put a check mark in the box next to the question.

☐   1. Did I indent each paragraph?

☐   2. Does each sentence tell one complete thought?

☐   3. Did I end each sentence with the correct mark?

☐   4. Did I begin each sentence with a capital letter?

☐   5. Did I use capital letters correctly in other places?

☐   6. Did I use commas correctly?

☐   7. Did I spell all the words the right way?

Are there other problem areas you should watch for? Make your own proofreading checklist.

☐ _____

☐ _____

☐ _____

☐ _____

☐ _____

☐ _____

☐ _____

☐ _____

Mark	Explanation	Examples
¶	Begin a new paragraph. Indent the paragraph.	¶We went to an air show last Saturday. Eight jets flew across the sky in the shape of V's, X's, and diamonds.
∧	Add letters, words, or sentences.	The leaves were red ∧and orange.
✄	Take out words, sentences, and punctuation marks. Correct spelling.	The sky is bright blew. (blue) Huge clouds, move quickly.
/	Change a capital letter to a small letter.	The Fireflies blinked in the dark.
≡	Change a small letter to a capital letter.	New York city is exciting.

_____

_____

_____

_____

_____

_____

_____

_____

_____

_____

_____

_____

_____

_____

_____

_____

_____

_____

_____